STOP LOSING CUSTOMERS

Transform your business, life, and profits by getting customers to stay longer, spend more, and cheerfully refer!

DEDICATION

—

Mariah Buck: You're such an amazing mom to our boys! Thank you.

Brandon Buck: You are an amazing man, and I am honored to be your dad.

Tyler, Jeremiah, Alexander, and Kellen Buck: You four have no idea how proud I am of all of you and how much joy you bring to my life daily. Thank you.

Tasha Hussey: Thank you for all you've done to love and support me this year.

Karli McNamee: You are literally the best human I know, and I appreciate you more than I'll ever be able to put into words.

Jared Smith: Thank you for the love and support.

Mandy Legarreta: You do so much for all of us at The Newsletter Pro. You truly are invaluable. Thank you.

The Newsletter Pro Family: I don't even have words for how much I appreciate each and every one of you. You work so hard and care so much, and it is my honor to work with you all.

There were at least a dozen other people I could have thanked. To all of my friends and family, I hope you know how much I love and appreciate you.

TABLE OF CONTENTS

USE IT OR LOSE IT:
HOW TO GET THE MOST OUT OF THIS BOOK

—

By reading "Stop Losing Customers" cover to cover, you're already guaranteed to learn a lot. Chapter by chapter, I'll guide you through what the relationship economy is, why it matters for your marketing efforts, and how you can use it to your advantage to decrease churn, increase referrals, bring in more customers, and make your office a happier, healthier work environment.

But, if all you do is read this book, then you won't get the full bang for your buck. If you want to keep your customers, grow your business, and improve your relationships, you need to actually take action on the lessons I've compiled here. I promise, if I didn't think that these things were worth doing, I wouldn't be writing about them. Every step that I recommend in this book is one that I've taken myself with The Newsletter Pro, and every single one has paid off!

To help you get the most out of "Stop Losing Customers" — in other words, to ensure that you use this knowledge and don't lose it — I've added some homework at the end of each chapter. Now, don't freak out on me; it's easy homework! And it's homework that will help you make money, which is more than any high school handout ever did for me.

Each chapter in the book ends with a vital question for you to consider. For example, "Is your business set up to adapt, or are you flirting with business failure?" If you struggle with answering the questions, don't worry — that's perfectly normal! That's why the end of each chapter also directs you to StopLosingCustomersBook.com/Resources, where you can find a handy roundup of resources I'm calling Steps to Success.

Those resources (like books, articles, blog posts, documentaries, and videos, including additional content from yours truly) give you instructions on how to take that chapter's lessons to the next level. Each suggestion should help deepen your understanding of the lesson and give you an even better idea of how it applies to your business. Sure, you don't HAVE to research See's Candies, check out John Boccuzzi, Jr.'s TED talk, or watch "FYRE: The Greatest Party That Never Happened" on Netflix, but if doing it will help you keep more customers, why not at least give it a shot?

If you'd rather not pause in your reading to check them out as you go, just visit the website when you're done with the book! Or, better yet, go there now and bookmark the page so that you can return to it when you're done with each chapter. Everything you need is just a click away.

Below each question and the web address, you'll also see a section called Action Steps where I've left some space for you to pencil in your notes. As soon as you finish the chapter, while the content is still fresh in your mind, you can use this spot to jot down your thoughts, ideas, and questions. This section is all about you, so use it however you'd like!

Personally, I've found taking notes while I read to be extremely helpful. I can flip back through them to remind myself what I've learned and what I still need to follow up on. If you're not a notetaker, I encourage you to at least grab a highlighter and mark up the sections of the book that hit home for you or that talk about something your company could work on. Your future self will thank you!

Now that you know what to expect and how to set yourself up for success, I think you're ready to tackle "Stop Losing Customers" for real. Just turn the page to get started!

CHAPTER 1:
ADAPT OR DIE: WHAT IS THE RELATIONSHIP ECONOMY?

—

From the '70s until the late '90s, we all lived and operated in a mass market economy. During that time, a select few controlled what we got and who we got it from. The same select few controlled the flow of information. Want to know about that new, fancy gadget you saw in an ad? Well, let's get a salesperson to give you that info. Want to know what others thought about a product or how it compares to the competition? Too bad. The attitude of many companies was, "Either buy from us on our terms or take a hike. After all, the customers need us more than we need them."

All of that changed in the late '90s as the internet started to take hold and become part of our daily lives. By that point, you could research a company, know how others felt about that company, compare competitors, and/or even compare pricing to make sure you got a good deal.

Many companies were caught off guard and unprepared for the power to shift from a select few to the consumer. Many of those companies didn't adapt and eventually went out of business. Additionally, with the shift in power came intense price competitions. It was literally a race to the bottom. Another group of companies that simply couldn't compete on price went under.

"The era we have entered now is called the relationship economy, and in order to thrive within it, you need to alter your entire understanding of how customer service works."

Today, we're in the middle of another shift where price is no longer the primary driver behind many purchasing decisions. Instead, relationships with the brand and the overall brand experience drive many purchase decisions, and that is especially good news for you and me. The era we have entered now is called the relationship economy, and in order to thrive within it, you need to alter your entire understanding of how customer service works.

You and I can't compete on price with the Walmarts or Amazons of the world. Heck, many of us can't even compete on price with some of our local competitors, which is why it's a good thing we have moved into the relationship economy. In the relationship economy, we don't have to compete solely on price. To be clear, I'm not suggesting you can gouge people, as that would clearly violate any relationship goodwill you've built up, but customers have made it clear that they are willing to pay more for great service and relationships.

Small business has always had the ability to be more personalized, more nimble, and create a better overall experience than big, slow, and oftentimes mismanaged companies, which naturally gives us the upper hand in this new economy. The problem is many small businesses have not taken advantage of their edge, but the ones that do have become immensely successful, despite what other companies have told them.

Let's take The Newsletter Pro, for instance. If you know anything about me, then you know I am the founder and CEO of The Newsletter Pro, but in the beginning, I didn't know if the company really would be successful because of the myths I'd been fed from the old mass market economy.

Back in 2011, before The Newsletter Pro was anything but an ambition I was pursuing, I was stuck in traffic and put in a CD of a business interview. It was all about the rise of e-books. While listening to the interview, the speaker noted that e-books had just out-sold physical books for the first time ever. They then went on to say how the world was changing and that everything was going digital. According to him, books, and print in general, would soon be a thing of the past.

This news was a big deal for me at the time. You see, in January 2011, I was 32 years old and had just started a new company called The Newsletter Pro; our objective was to create custom print newsletters for other businesses. Later that evening, after I put the boys to bed (I have five kiddos and they are all boys), I decided to do some more research into the rise of e-books and the impending fall of physical books. Search result after search result painted a very gloomy picture for print.

If it seems odd to you that a 32-year-old would start a print newsletter company in 2011, that's because it is odd. I have a philosophy I live by: When the masses are all going in one direction, I look to the opposite direction, as I've found the masses are nearly always wrong. Of course, even a blind squirrel finds a nut now and again, but by and large, I don't like to follow everyone else.

Before starting The Newsletter Pro, when I looked around, I noticed all of my friends starting online companies. Some were offering social media help, website development, or SEO services, and they were encouraging me to do the same.

Instead, I followed my philosophy, and I went in the exact opposite direction with print newsletters, but that wasn't by chance. I knew they worked from past experience and knew they were a ton of hard work to create each month. I figured it would be better to play in the smaller pond of print newsletters than it would be to play in the bloody ocean that is the digital marketing niche.

Sitting in traffic in my car, listening to the interviewee talk about the rise of e-books, I was second-guessing my decision. In that moment, I felt like I'd just made a huge mistake. Days earlier, I had just agreed to buy a $5,000 piece of equipment to help get my new business off the ground, and I was getting that $5,000 from my personal savings account. Then, on that day, according to the data on e-book sales and this expert, print is dead!?

After my initial fears subsided, I told myself there is no way print is going to die. It's been around for thousands of years. I did a bit more research and didn't find a single ray of hope.

Was the sky really falling? Was I about to make the biggest mistake of my life? Maybe my friends were right. Maybe I should go into the SEO and website development business ... websites aren't going anywhere anytime soon.

But I knew how well newsletters worked; after all, I'd been sending one every month for my companies since 2002, and they worked for me. I reasoned with myself: If they worked for so long for me, why would they stop working now?

In the back of my mind, I was still scared I was making a massive mistake that could ruin my family, but logically, I knew the media was wrong. Businesses don't stop using marketing tactics that work and make them money.

It was hard to ignore the fear and self-doubt, but ultimately, I did ignore it all and pushed on. Going against the flow had worked for me in the past, and I wasn't going to stop then. Thankfully, I was right and my business is thriving ... phew. As I write this, I have 68-plus employees, and my company sends millions of print and digital newsletters every year.

During our first year in sales, we made $102,000. Not exactly lighting the world on fire, but we were growing. By the middle of 2012, our monthly sales were up to about $35,000 per month, and I had hired the first employee for The Newsletter Pro. By the end of 2012, we were doing $85,000 per month in sales, a run rate of $1,020,000.

By the start of 2013, The Newsletter Pro really started to grow; we had our marketing moving in the right direction. I was doing all the selling, and we had a team to do the newsletter project management, writing, editing, design, printing, and mailing. Our growth didn't seem to let up. No joke, I remember sitting on the phone for eight hours a day on sales phone calls for six weeks straight. The only time I got a break was if someone didn't show up. I literally had to tell prospects that we were so busy with new customers that if they didn't buy on this call, it would be their responsibility to follow up with us. I know, horrible salesmanship on my part, but we had so many one-call closes that my onboarding team couldn't handle more new clients.

As The Newsletter Pro grew, we started to win numerous awards. We've been on Inc. magazine's Inc. 500 list twice (it would have been three times, but one year, I was so busy that I forgot to apply). We also made the Inc. 5000, received the Entrepreneur 360 award given out by Entrepreneur magazine, and have been named one of the best places to work in Idaho for four years in a row. Personally, I've taught tens of thousands of entrepreneurs about relationship marketing, business growth, and creating an amazing culture, among other topics.

Making the shift to be a relationship-focused business is the reason for my success today, but don't just take it from me. My industry isn't the only one that started thriving once industry leaders started to alter their business model to one that prioritized customer relationships.

Remember in 2011 when all the media could talk about was the death of print books and the rise of e-books?
According to a recent article in Forbes, independent bookstores have made a huge resurgence.

People of all ages love having a place to go grab a cup of coffee and discover new authors and books that they'd likely never come across in the digital world.

Customers enjoy in-store experiences, like snatching the newest science-fiction book off the top shelf or getting their favorite nonfiction book personally signed by the author. Many find value in interacting with passionate staff members who always have the best recommendations.

The bookstore's transformation from a cluttered room with a bunch of obscure books to a relationship- and experience-driven destination has allowed the number of independent bookstores to grow by over 35% since 2009, and the number of new independent bookstores continues to grow each month.

How'd they do it? How did a business category many of us thought was simply not going to make it not only come out alive but also fight back?

It all boils down to the customer experience.

Think about it: In most cases, it's much more convenient and even cheaper to buy from Amazon. The alternative is getting in the car, driving to the store, finding parking, going into the store, finding the book you want, paying for it, leaving the store, and getting back into the car. That's a lot of work, and depending on how you drive, there is possibly even some risk involved. With all that is required to go to a bookstore to get a book, why are independent bookstores thriving?

Here's the answer, and it's simpler than you think: They figured out how to beat Amazon ... not on price but on feelings. They win because of how people feel when they engage all of their senses in the store. They can touch the books and feel the paper as they flip through the pages. They hear the hushed whispers of people talking softly as they discover new stories. Going to the bookstore has transformed from simply buying a book and become as much about the relationships with the staff and the experiences they create for their customers as it is about the books themselves.

Think about what these independent bookstores have done. After all, a book is just a commodity. You can buy them anywhere, and they're all the same. It's not like you get a bonus chapter if you get the book at Amazon over the local independent bookstore or Barnes & Noble store.

Independent bookstores should still be a dying business but instead, they're growing. That is the power of relationships and experience in this economy. That is also the power of being a relationship marketer.

If relationship marketing can change the fortune of independent bookstores, what can it do for your industry? How can it help you grow and thrive when you don't have to resurrect an industry and simply need to beat the local competitors? How can it take a commoditized product or service and make it stand out from the competition?
If we do have to take on the Amazons of the world, like the independent bookstore has, how do we not only survive but also thrive?

That is exactly what we're going to explore in this book. I'll give you the tools you need to be a master of marketing in the relationship economy, but there is one thing I can't give you in this book to help you along the journey: passion.

When we talk about relationships and experience-based marketing, you have to actually be willing to build relationships with prospects, customers, referral partners, and your employees ... and you actually have to care. Care about their success, their problems, and how they feel. If you don't care, if you are doing all this relationship building and experience creation just to make a buck, everyone will see right through you. It won't keep customers from leaving your business; in fact, it will likely accelerate the loss of customers as they quickly realize you're not genuine.

But, if you really do care — if you really do want your customers to have an amazing experience, if you really want your customers to get the most value out of what you offer — then focusing on the customer experience, building relationships, and customer success will pay huge dividends, the kind your competitors can only dream of.

As you dive into the book, I'll share tools, tips, and tactics you can use to help you build better relationships with your employees, customers, and vendors. By building relationships, you'll quickly notice a decrease in customer churn and employee churn, both of which will increase your bottom line and make your job as CEO easier. Ultimately, this book will show you how to thrive as an entrepreneur in the relationship economy.

Let's get started.

**IS YOUR BUSINESS SET UP TO ADAPT,
OR ARE YOU FLIRTING WITH BUSINESS FAILURE?**

Visit **www.stoplosingcustomersbook.com/resources**
for follow-up steps to success.

ACTION STEPS TO SET UP YOUR BUSINESS TO ADAPT:

_____

_____

_____

_____

_____

_____

_____

_____

_____

CHAPTER 2:
THE CASE FOR RELATIONSHIP MARKETING

—

Let me give you an example of relationship marketing in action.

A few months ago, I met a doctor at a show I was speaking at. I got on stage and gave my presentation and ended up in the back of the room taking questions. A few hours later, one of my employees texted me and asked me to come by the booth. They said one of the attendees wanted to ask me a few questions. I headed to the convention hall, introduced myself, and this prospect and I started chatting.

The prospect was a dentist with a successful thriving practice. We started talking about how to build relationships and get more referrals. I showed her the newsletters and told her how we make them custom for each client, match her practice's branding, etc. The dentist asked me about one of our quasi-competitors. (I say "quasi" because we're the only company on a large scale that creates custom newsletters; everyone else is either 100% template or some version of a templated newsletter or the company creating custom newsletters just makes them as a side gig.) Forty-five minutes later, the dentist decides to join The Newsletter Pro family. The next day, I was getting ready to head to the airport, and I get a text from my team again asking me to come to the booth. I head over, and who do I see but the dentist from the previous day. She tells me she loves the product and thinks it would be great for her practice, but she has been using a templated competitor of ours for years, and that competitor is her neighbor. She said she doesn't love their product but after considering it that evening, she felt bad at the thought of having to cancel the newsletter her neighbor creates for her. She then said she doesn't think she can switch to us.

Of course, I totally understand how she feels and why she decided to stay with this quasi-competitor.

Think about that story for a second. Her relationship with the neighbor/ my quasi-competitor ended up being so strong that even after she had technically switched and bought from The Newsletter Pro, on second thought, she couldn't pull the trigger.

It's hard to be neighbors with all your customers, but with relationship marketing, you can achieve a similar outcome. You can practically build a fence around your customers, making them immune to the siren song of your competitors, who would cheerfully steal all your customers and figuratively cut your throat, given the opportunity.

Do you see the opportunity? Can you imagine how amazing your business will be when you've built relationships with your customers and won their loyalty? Think about how this can change your business for the better. How much more smoothly will your business run with a relationship mindset? How much lower will churn be? How many more deals can you close?

The reality of the world we live in today is nearly all of us sell commoditized products or services.

Think about it like this: In the U.S. alone, there are ...

- 130,000 dentists (That's 16 dentists for every Starbucks in the U.S.)
- 400,000-plus small or solo law firms
- 204,000 licensed physical therapists
- 556,000 plumbers

I could go on, but you get the picture. It may not always feel like you sell a commodity, but the vast majority of us do. Even if you serve local clients, they have options.

For example, my dad lives in Napa Valley in California but goes to a dentist here in Idaho. He comes out and visits 2–4 times per year, and twice a year while he is here, he sees my dentist. Of course, most people won't go out of state for a service like dentistry, but they still have nearly limitless choices in and around where they live.

How do we overcome being just a commodity and stand out from the competition? Most people try to do it with features or perceived benefits that don't matter and won't help. Even if you have a unique benefit, your competitors can copy it or get close enough to copying it that your prospects are confused. Your new whiz-bang benefit may not be a benefit your customers care about.

Many entrepreneurs don't even understand what a benefit to the customer is. You can see it in their marketing.

"We have the friendliest staff in the valley!" Not according to that last Google review. It says your front desk person is horrible, which, by the way, is one of the most common issues with small businesses. I can tell you it costs businesses billions annually. When was the last time you secret-shopped the people who answer calls for you?

"I've been treating patients for 22 years and counting." Who cares? Maybe your techniques are now antiquated or your office and equipment are outdated. How long you've been in business matters exactly zero. Many times, the longer you've been in business, the worse the experience is.

"We have the best prices in town." Okay, so I should expect a Walmart level of service? You have the lowest prices in town, but what about online? No small business wins a price war.

"We're full service!" As opposed to other businesses that only give you half a service? Most of the time, I don't even know what the entrepreneur means when they say this. If I need my brakes fixed, I couldn't care less that you can also replace my muffler. Many times I'd rather just go to the place that only does brakes; they're likely better at it than the full-service people.

Some entrepreneurs simply provide a list of services or products they offer and then consider that good marketing. For example:

- Auto Glass Repair & Replace
- Residential Screens & Glass
- Commercial Storefront and Glass
- Insulated Units

Okay, great, you provide that service along with everyone else in your industry.

One of the many issues with these examples is that no one cares about any of the "benefits" I just listed out, but somehow, millions of small businesses still advertise like this. Even if you lead with services, odds are your competition has the same services, and they can buy the same or similar products. They can get matching equipment or keep the same store hours. They can copy your ad almost word for word ... even if it is lame. Personally, when I see that, it always makes me laugh; it's like the blind following the blind.

So, what is it that your competitors can't copy? They can't copy *you* or *your team*. Think about this. Your competitors can steal campaigns, they can steal ideas, they can add similar product lines, and they can even take an employee every now and again, but the one thing they can't do is be you. They can't tell your stories, they don't have your personality, they don't have your skills, and they can't take the whole team. Being you and letting that shine through so you can attract other like-minded customers who are there for you and are fans of yours will have a massive impact on your business. The other benefit to relationship-based marketing is that you tend to repel those who aren't be a good fit for you.

Let's pretend for a second: How would your business be different if you had a personal relationship with EVERY customer?

Start off by thinking about a few of the people you do service for who you have personal relationships with. No, I don't mean the freeloaders like your brother-in-law, but real customers who you know from the business and have a relationship with.

Got someone in mind? Good. If I came into your marketplace and opened a competing business, how difficult would it be for me to steal that customer?

Nearly impossible, right?

Can you imagine if all your customers felt that way?
How would that change your business?
What would that do to the number of lost customers you have each month?
How much more revenue would you make because everyone would simply take your advice on what is best for them because they trust you?

Let me ask you this question: Do you think those loyal people who you have relationships with would refer more business to you, or less?

What if you could create an experience that would get customers to use your goods or services just two more times per year than they currently do? Would that amount to more or less business for you? Could you find an upsell at least some of them need and sell that to them while they're in your store?

Of course it all would mean more: more sales, more referrals, more growth, and more profits.

If you want to decrease churn and make more money, you have to focus on fostering loyalty and long-term engagement with customers and prospects instead of focusing on singular transactions.

Play the long game. Know the real profit is in the long-term relationship, not short-term gain.

Know that providing an amazing experience is the difference between being a commodity — being oversubscribed — and being irreplaceable.

Believe that churn is evil and the killer of profits and growth for any company. The best companies closely monitor churn, as it is an indicator of issues in customer relationships and customer experience.

The best companies give a damn about their team, their customers, and their community.

If you want continued growth and real success, not the BS fake success you see on Facebook or Instagram, you *must* transform into a relationship marketer. You *must* focus on having amazing employees, and you *must* focus on lowering customer churn.

The good news is that relationship marketing makes all of that possible.

My goal is to turn you into a master relationship marketer. When this happens, you'll have customers who love you and your company and will cheerfully refer friends and family members. You'll have a company so focused on the customer relationship and experience that your customers wouldn't even consider doing business with a competitor. A company whose customers are in your corner should someone attack you offline or online. A company that releases new products or services and has a line of people who are waiting to buy what you sell. If that sounds good to you, you're in the right place and bought the right book.

WHAT IS IT THAT MAKES YOU *YOU*?

Visit **www.stoplosingcustomersbook.com/resources**
for follow-up steps to success.

ACTION STEPS FOR LETTING YOUR *YOU* SHINE THROUGH:

_____

_____

_____

_____

_____

_____

_____

_____

_____

CHAPTER 3:
THE SILENT KILLER OF PROFITS AND BUSINESS GROWTH

—

This is possibly the most important chapter you'll ever read in a business book. I know that's a bold statement, but when you get what I'm teaching in this chapter right, it will change your business and life for the better.

It is sexy to talk about getting new customers. In fact, I almost didn't put this chapter here. For a brief moment, I was even tempted to put the new customer acquisition section of this book first, but that's not where anyone should start when creating their relationship marketing strategy. Had I moved chapters and put the "more" exciting new customer acquisition chapter first, I would not be a good relationship marketer because that would not be in your best interest.

The place where every relationship marketer should start is at the end.

It may not be the sexiest way, but with all the extra profit you make from fixing this problem, you can buy yourself something nice to make up for it.

Most businesses' customers are abandoning ship like they're on the Titanic, and the business has no clue it's happening.

Fixing this issue is one of the single largest opportunities for growth, in terms of sales and profits, for any business. Let's take a deep dive into the problem, so we can strategize a solution.

To fix our churn problem, we first need to know how bad the problem is because churn is the silent killer of businesses. In my opinion, entrepreneurs don't like to think about churn because it is bad news ... losing customers is never good. Also, calculating your churn is one of the most difficult numbers for small businesses to figure out. I saw a study recently that said over two-thirds of businesses have no idea how many customers they lose each month. Two-thirds! That's crazy town.

If you fall into the two-thirds category, you *must* start to monitor your churn number at least monthly.

The first time most businesses even take note of a churn issue is when the business hits a plateau. If the business survives their churn issues — which is a big "if" for many businesses — they will hit a point where they have as many customers jumping ship as they have new customers. I've found it actually takes most businesses 12 months of not growing or even going backward before they even realize there is a problem. Churn is actually one of the primary reasons the business failure rate is so high.

Let me share an example with you. I do a lot of marketing for dentists and know that according to the American Dental Association, the average dentist loses 27 patients per month, or about 12%–15% of their total patient base per year. Unfortunately for dentists, based on data from over 13,000 U.S. dentists who use Sikka Software, the average number of new patients per month is only 20. Houston, we have a problem!

I'm not a math wizard or anything, but even using common core math to calculate the answer, it appears the average dentist is losing seven more patients than they bring into the practice each month. That nets out to a loss of 84 patients per year. With the average patient spending about $2,000 per year at the dentist, that amounts to about $168,000 in lost revenue in a single year. Personally, I feel that is a bad business plan.

The unfortunate reality is that I've met very few people and even fewer dentists who actually know how many customers — or, in the case of dentistry, patients — they lose each month. To be fair, many people don't even know how many new customers they bring in each month either. Both of those numbers are very important.

If you think the above numbers are bad, they are, but it's about to get worse.

According to a survey of my dental clients, they spend on average $250–$350 per new patient. So, they'd have to spend about $21,000 (number of additional patients needed (84) times cost per patient ($250) equals $21,000) on additional marketing, not to grow but to simply break even.

That marketing spend is money coming straight off the bottom line. Now, the average dental office does a horrible job of turning a new patient into a loyal patient. It is estimated that 41% of the patients who come in for a first visit won't be back for a second one. That means we don't actually have to spend $21,000 on new patient marketing to break even; we have to spend over $35,500[1] just to get back to even.

---

[1] 142 total patients needed if 41% don't come back for a second visit.
142 multiplied by $250 equals $35,500 in marketing spend.

Of course, the average dentist (and most other companies in America) go negative on that first visit due to some discount or promo they're running to attract new customers or patients. That further increases the above loss and means 100% of that expense impacts your profits.

If you thought that it couldn't get any worse, I'm sorry to say you're wrong.

You see, as you lose customers, you do see a change in what are known as variable costs. To continue with our dental example, they pay the hygienist a percentage of the revenue from cleaning your teeth. They also have some supplies that are disposable. As they lose patients, those expenses decrease, which is nice. But every business also has what are called fixed expenses, and fixed expenses don't go down due to a decrease in patients. For example, your rent is a fixed expense; insurance for the building and the phone and internet bills are all fixed expenses too. A portion of your fixed expenses has to be allocated to each patient in this case. So, as you lose patients, you're actually making every other patient you have less profitable because every lost patient's fixed expenses have to now be divided up among the remaining patients.

Losing customers is literally a downward spiral and routinely kills businesses. Is it starting to make sense why this churn number is so important to the long-term health of your business?

If you truly want to scale, you have to know, monitor, and work to improve your company's churn number. If you don't, you're playing a very dangerous game and are at risk of waking up one day and having your business in real trouble.

Why Aren't More People Aware of the Churn Issue in Business?

A study done by the Rockefeller Group found that 68% of customers leave a company not because of price but because the customers feel the company is indifferent to them. Most entrepreneurs don't realize they have an issue for a variety of reasons, but the most common reason is they simply don't track churn, and they accept the most common reason people give for leaving, which is price or money. Either I found a cheaper price or I don't have any money to buy from you. The good news is that now you're aware that customers are lying in order to save face, not hurt your feelings. I know I've used price or money as an excuse before, but it wasn't a determining factor. It's rare that price is the reason I started looking for a new provider.

Source: The Rockefeller Group

Now that we know indifference is the No. 1 reason someone leaves, not price, I want to ask this: Are you indifferent to your customers? Do you care if they have a good experience or a good outcome with your product or service? Do you care if they come back again or not?

Of course you do. Your customers are literally the people who put food on your table. They help you pay your bills and take vacations. They are the reason your kids can go to private school or you can buy that new sports car. Without your customers, you're out of business and have to do the unthinkable — get a job!

I know you don't feel indifferent to or about your customers. The simple fact that you're reading this book tells me that. So, why do so many of the customers who leave your business feel like you do?

I'm a big believer that actions speak louder than words, so let's look at our actions, or lack thereof, that may be causing customers to feel like we're indifferent to them.

The first step is to look at your communication with customers. Start by listing out all the ways you communicate with your customers currently.

An average business communication strategy looks something like this.

1. We send emails about four times per month with promotional offers.
2. We send a bill once per month.
3. We remind them that their appointment is coming via generic email and text messages.
4. We post funny industry memes on Facebook and Instagram.

5. We call them if their bill is past due or if they miss an appointment.
6. We make small talk when they come in.

Can you tell me what's wrong with this small-business communication strategy?

"The business is a narcissist."

All the communication is about the business. Every interaction with the customer, with the exception of No. 6, was all focused on the business and the needs of the business. The business wants you, the customer, to buy more. The business wants you to pay your bill. The business wants you to come back and buy this new item that is now on sale. The business wants to take the customer's social media time to talk about — what else? — the business's wants, needs, or industry. The business is a narcissist.

The business is communicating that it only cares about itself and not about the other person in the relationship. It is no wonder that 68% of consumers say they leave a business because they feel the business is indifferent to them; the business *is* indifferent to them.

We can all sit around and claim we care, but, like I said earlier, actions speak louder than words, and our actions say we don't care about anyone but ourselves.

IS YOUR BUSINESS A NARCISSIST?

Visit **www.stoplosingcustomersbook.com/resources** for follow-up steps to success.

ACTION STEPS TO SHOW YOU CARE ABOUT YOUR CONSUMER:

_____

_____

_____

_____

_____

_____

_____

_____

_____

CHAPTER 4:
HOW TO ACCURATELY CALCULATE CHURN FOR YOUR BUSINESS

—

Believe it or not, there are many ways to calculate churn. The vast majority of small businesses don't need to get fancy with this calculation, but there are three different churn numbers you need to calculate.

Monthly Churn: This is the number of lost customers at the end of a period divided by the total number of customers at the start of the period.

The calculation looks like this:

15 / 500 = 3%

Here is a more detailed example: On Jan. 1, you have 500 customers. At the end of the business day on Jan. 31, you have 485 customers, not including any new customers you signed up. Your lost customer total is 15. In this scenario, your churn rate would be 3% that month. If during the month of January you added 25 new customers, on Feb. 1, your starting number for calculating churn would be 510 customers.

This is a super simple method of calculating churn, but it is accurate. You can use this method for calculating daily, weekly, monthly, quarterly, or annual churn.

Here is another example assuming you want to calculate daily churn. 15 / 500 = 0.03 or 3%

3% / 31 = 0.0967 churn per day

Now that we know our customer churn number, we need to look at our gross revenue churn number.

Revenue Churn: This is the amount of lost revenue in a given period due to cancellations and downgrades. Calculating revenue churn is also simple.

You take the total lost revenue in a period and divide it by the total revenue at the start of the period.

The calculation looks like this:

$4,000 / $100,000 = 0.04 or 4%

Now, you'll notice in the above scenario that the actual revenue churn is greater as a percentage than the previous example of customer churn. This happens when you have a downgrade program in place where a customer calls and doesn't cancel but lowers their total spending with you.

If you currently don't have a downgrade option in place in your business, getting one in place needs to be a huge priority. Many times when a customer cancels, the cancellation may not have anything to do with your product or service; it may simply be a budget issue. Having an option to keep the customer in the fold but help them spend less money, likely for fewer services or fewer products, is a great way to reduce both customer churn and revenue churn and make more money in the long run.

The final churn number you need to know, and one that I'm always very focused on, is net revenue churn.

Net Revenue Churn: This is the total amount of lost revenue in a period. It is calculated by any upsells to existing customers in the period divided by the total revenue at the start of the period. Let me do the math for you below.

$4,000 (revenue churn) - $2,500 (upsells) = $1,500 in lost revenue / $100,000 (total sales) = .015 or 1.5% net revenue churn.

If these numbers were from a real business, I'd say this business is doing pretty good overall. Despite $4,000 in lost revenue from cancellations and downsells, they were still able to add $2,500 in upsells, taking their net revenue churn down to 1.5%. My personal goal for net revenue churn is 0%. The job of a customer success manager is to find upsells that will be beneficial to both the customers and the company and close those deals.

World-class companies will actually have a positive net revenue churn number, where the total number of upsells is greater than the cancellations, actually allowing the upsells to grow the business even before you sign on a single new customer. How cool is that?

Using our above company as an example, think about all the things they could do to get their net revenue churn number to zero.

"Once they have the data, they are now in a position to effect change."

They could work to improve their downsell process and offerings. They could work on customer communication and relationship marketing. They could work on the upsell process or add an additional product or service their customers may want/need. I could go on, but you get the point. Once they have the data, they are now in a position to effect change. If the actions they took got them to just neutral revenue churn, where they brought in as much in upsells as they lost in downsells and cancellations, how much faster would they grow? How much more profit would they make? Let's take a look.

We know our hypothetical company has an average monthly customer spend of $200. We also know they're growing at 5% per month, which is great. Unfortunately, they have a 3% monthly churn rate. We also know that their revenue churn is a bit high since they are losing 15 customers per month and the average customer spends $200 per month. It appears they should only be losing $3,000 in revenue per month, but since they're losing $4,000 per month, we can assume they have a downgrade program that some customers are choosing over outright canceling.

Let's first look at our hypothetical company as if they didn't take any action to upsell or improve churn. I'm going to list their net numbers after churn is subtracted for each month in this hypothetical year. The chart on the next page assumes that this business will continue to add 25 new customers per month. Note: I chose not to make this number a 5% growth rate because I've found marketing for most companies simply doesn't scale like that. It is far more realistic that they average the same number of customers each month over the year than gradually scaling their marketing efforts.

Churn In Your Business

Churn - Is the number of lost customers at the end of a month divided by the total number of customers at the start of the period.

Company A

$15/500 = 3\%$ $200/MONTH   GROWING 5%
AVERAGE SPEND

Month	Customers	Churn %	Lost Customers	New Customers	Total Customers	Upsells	Revenue
Jan	500	3	15	25	510		$102.000
Feb	510	3	15	25	520		$103,940
Mar	520	3	16	25	529		$105,822
Apr	529	3	16	25	538		$107,647
May	538	3	16	25	547		$109,418
Jun	547	3	16	25	556		$111,135
Jul	556	3	17	25	564		$112,801
Aug	564	3	17	25	572		$114,417
Sept	572	3	17	25	580		$115,985
Oct	580	3	17	25	588		$117,505
Nov	588	3	18	25	595		$118,980
Dec	595	3	18	25	602		$120,411
			Annual Lost Customers	Annual New Customers	Annual Customers		Annual Sales
Totals			198	300	602		$1,340,060

Now, let's look at this business as if they were able to execute on the plan earlier in this chapter and get to all the way down to $1,500 in net revenue churn.

UPSELLS

Month	Customers	Churn %	Lost Customers	New Customers	Total Customers	Upsells	Revenue
Jan	500	3	15	25	510	$2,500	$104,500
Feb	510	3	15	25	520	$2,550	$108,990
Mar	520	3	16	25	529	$2,599	$113,470
Apr	529	3	16	25	538	$2,646	$117,941
May	538	3	16	25	547	$2,691	$122,403
Jun	547	3	16	25	556	$2,735	$126,856
Jul	556	3	17	25	564	$2,778	$131,300
Aug	564	3	17	25	572	$2,778	$131,300
Sept	572	3	17	25	580	$2,860	$140,164
Oct	580	3	17	25	588	$2,900	$139,206
Nov	588	3	18	25	595	$2,938	$148,997
Dec	595	3	18	25	602	$2,974	$153,402
			Annual Lost Customers	Annual New Customers	Annual Customers	Upsell Revenue	Annual Sales
Totals			198	300	602	$32,991	$1,542,965

As you can see, just by focusing on customer success in the form of upsells, we can add over $200,000 in new sales over a 12-month period. The good news is that it is very likely the new sales are actually super profitable because upsells tend to be more profitable products for most companies. If that holds true for your business, then all the extra profit is simply an added bonus.

Now, what would happen if we also decreased churn just a little? After all, 33% annual churn is pretty high. Let's look at a reduction down to 20% and 25%.

25% DECREASE IN CHURN

Month	Customers	Churn %	Lost Customers	New Customers	Total Customers	Upsells	Revenue
Jan	500	2.1	11	25	515	$2,500	$105,400
Feb	515	2.1	11	25	529	$2,573	$110,812
Mar	529	2.1	11	25	543	$2,643	$116,235
Apr	543	2.1	11	25	556	$2,713	$121,669
May	556	2.1	12	25	570	$2,781	$127,114
Jun	570	2.1	12	25	583	$2,848	$132,569
Jul	583	2.1	12	25	595	$2,913	$138,035
Aug	595	2.1	13	25	608	$2,977	$143,512
Sept	608	2.1	13	25	620	$3,039	$148,998
Oct	620	2.1	13	25	632	$3,100	$148,915
Nov	632	2.1	13	25	644	$3,160	$159,999
Dec	644	2.1	14	25	655	$3,219	$165,514
			Annual Lost Customers	Annual New Customers	Annual Customers	Upsells	Annual Sales
Totals			145	300	655	$34,465	$1,618,771

20% DECREASE IN CHURN

Month	Customers	Churn %	Lost Customers	New Customers	Total Customers	Upsells	Revenue
Jan	500	1.67	8	25	517	$2,500	$105,830
Feb	517	1.67	9	25	533	$2,583	$111,688
Mar	533	1.67	9	25	549	$2,665	$117,572
Apr	549	1.67	9	25	565	$2,746	$123,484
May	565	1.67	9	25	581	$2,825	$129,422
Jun	581	1.67	10	25	596	$2,903	$135,385
Jul	596	1.67	10	25	611	$2,979	$141,375
Aug	611	1.67	10	25	626	$3,054	$147,389
Sept	626	1.67	10	25	640	$3,128	$153,427
Oct	640	1.67	11	25	655	$3,201	$153,810
Nov	655	1.67	11	25	669	$3,273	$165,576
Dec	669	1.67	11	25	682	$3,343	$171,686
			Annual Lost Customers	Annual New Customers	Annual Customers	Upsell Revenue	Annual Sales
Totals			118	300	682	$35,200	$1,656,644

At the lowest churn rate of 20%, our company now has a positive net revenue churn number and has $316,584 in additional annual sales.

The best part here is that the number doesn't really tell the whole story.

There is another number any fast-growing company looks at that really gives the complete picture here, and that number is the company's run rate. Your run rate is the total revenue sales at the end of a period — for example, total sales in December multiplied out by 12 months to see where the business is heading if you were able to maintain those sales for the next 12 months.

Let's see the run rate number in action.

If our company hadn't focused at all on churn and just kept plugging along, they would have a run rate of $120,411 x 12 = $1,444,932. (chart 1)

If we now look at the run rate from the 20% churn chart (chart 4), we see monthly sales in December of $171,686 x 12 = $2,060,232. That is an increase of $615,300 per year or 42.5%, which is crazy growth.

Had our company not focused on churn at all, the growth rate would have been only 11.67%, which is average at best.

If we dig further, we'll see that our company can accomplish a similar growth rate just by focusing on new customers.

NEW CUSTOMERS

Month	Customers	Churn %	Lost Customers	New Customers	Total Customers	Upsells	Revenue
Jan	500	3	15	47	532		$106,400
Feb	532	3	16	47	563		$112,608
Mar	563	3	17	47	593		$118,630
Apr	593	3	18	48	623		$124,671
May	623	3	19	48	653		$130,531
Jun	653	3	20	48	681		$136,215
Jul	681	3	20	48	709		$141,728
Aug	709	3	21	48	735		$147,077
Sept	735	3	22	48	761		$152,264
Oct	761	3	23	48	786		$157,296
Nov	786	3	24	48	811		$162,177
Dec	811	3	24	48	835		$166,912
			Annual Lost Customers	Annual New Customers	Annual Customers		Annual Sales
Totals			238	573	835		**$1,656,509**

You looked at those numbers and hopefully saw what I did: garbage.

In all the previous examples, you'll notice the average number of new customers gained each month was 25. In the chart above, you'll notice that we need 47–48 new customers per month to achieve a very similar growth rate but without the focus on churn reduction and upsells via customer success.

To go from 25 new customers per month on average to nearly double is not easy, as anyone who has ever owned a business can attest to. Plus, focusing on new customers in this scenario would also be less profitable. As you know, every new customer has a cost to acquire and onboard them. This cost per customer can easily be 4–12 months of average revenue. To put it another way, on the low end, our business would have to spend an additional $18,400 in marketing per month to get the extra new customers it needs to have similar sales as those in Chart 4.

Of course, engaging in relationship marketing and having a customer success employee has expenses attached to it, but it is typically between 15%–35% of what you would spend if you tried to get the same revenue through new customer acquisition. For our business to achieve the same growth shown in Chart 4, they'd spend only $6,440 per month in relationship marketing and customer success.

The numbers don't lie, and as you can see, focusing on reducing churn and helping your customers have more success is good for the customer, your business, and your bottom line.

I'll end with one additional comment here on one other huge factor you should consider: your business's resale value. I've bought numerous businesses over the years. Some were doing hundreds of thousands of dollars in sales per year, and my largest acquisition was doing $6 million in sales per year. A low churn number with a good customer success process can have a profound impact on sales. If we used our above company as an example and assumed it has a 20% profit margin, its resale value would climb between $412,040–$824,092. You may not be ready to sell today, but any business that is worth selling is a business worth owning. No one is giving you big dollars for a crap business. If you set your business up as if you were going to sell and try to get the maximum value out of it, by the time you're done putting everything in place, you'll have a great business that kicks out a ton of profit, and you may just decide to keep it.

Be Careful of Numbers That Are Too Good to Be True!

I have one more word of caution on churn, and it might actually be the most important one in this chapter. **If you get a number that appears too good to be true, it likely is.** World-class companies have a 10%–12% annual churn rate. For example, in 2016, Costco had 12% membership churn per year and they're world-class. Amazon Prime had 10%, and they're also world-class. My company averages 15% +/- per year. One of my buddies in the personal training franchise averages 35% per year, and his franchisees' churn is higher than the corporate stores. You should trust but verify any number you get. If you're a small business with a number less than 20% per year, you need to really dig deep and make sure that number is correct. One time I had an employee who was sandbagging the churn numbers to make sure they exceeded their goal to get a larger bonus at the end of the year. I've had a situation where churn was higher than normal, and my office manager didn't want to look bad, so they didn't do a thorough job figuring out the churn number. If the number is too low, it could also be that the data is just so bad that you or your office manager can't get an accurate number. If that is the issue, you'll likely have to dig in and manually figure out your company's churn.

Regardless of the situation, you need to be able to get an accurate number. Since every business has a churn issue, you don't need to have your churn number 100% nailed down before you take the next steps, but at a minimum, be in the process of getting accurate data.

DO YOU HAVE
A CHURN PROBLEM?

Visit **www.stoplosingcustomersbook.com/resources**
for follow-up steps to success.

ACTION STEPS TO MONITOR MONTHLY, REVENUE, AND
NET REVENUE CHURN:

_____

_____

_____

_____

_____

_____

_____

_____

_____

_____

CHAPTER 5:
AN OVERLOOKED BENEFIT TO BUILDING RELATIONSHIPS WITH CUSTOMERS: REFERRALS

—

You can throw all the money you want at your marketing campaigns. You can spend tens of thousands of dollars on branding, landing pages, funnels, Facebook ads, sales letters, and postcards. But the single best new customer is still a customer gained through referrals. According to a study conducted by The New York Times, 65% of companies' new business comes from referrals. And luckily, referrals are a natural byproduct of relationship marketing.

One of the best parts about getting a referral is that referred customers spend more than customers gained via cold media. A study done in 2011 by The American Marketing Association, involving over 10,000 customers at a well-known German bank, found that referred customers spent more on their first visit, stayed longer, and had an overall 16% higher lifetime value than non-referred customers.

So, how do you generate more customer referrals? Some people don't give it their all when going after referrals, and the reason they don't comes down to the fact that they just don't know how to encourage referrals.

Referrals come in a few different forms. The two most popular forms of referrals are word-of-mouth referrals and partner referrals.

Word-of-mouth referrals are the most basic. One person simply tells another person about your business, product, or service. Partner referrals come when an entity with a list or audience promotes your business, product, or service. For most businesses, word-of-mouth referrals can be the easiest to achieve ... if they're done right.

To successfully get a mass number of word-of-mouth referrals, you need to:

1. Serve your customers. Referrals start with how well your product or service serves the needs of your customers. This may seem obvious, but I can't tell you how many times I've gotten great service from the owner, only to have the front desk staff ruin any chance of a referral from me.

2. Motivate your customers. This is typically done using some kind of monetary reward, but it has to make an impact. Companies fail at this when they don't provide a reward with a high enough value. If you want more referrals, now is not the time to be cheap.

I'm often amazed that companies will pay hundreds of dollars for new leads via cold traffic but want to offer a $25 gas gift card for a referral. That's crazy. Contrary to popular belief, if you want to generate more referrals, it will require a significant investment of money on your part — though far, far less than you would spend going after brand new, non-referred customers.

Keep in mind that this isn't something you are "throwing money" at. This approach is very purposeful and something you absolutely need to track.

3. Recognize your customers. If you really want to kick your customer referrals into overdrive, find ways to publicly recognize those customers who have sent you the most referrals. Putting their picture on Facebook, on your office wall of fame, or in your newsletter are all good places to start.

Write an article about how amazing this person is. Thank them for their referrals in your newsletter. Give them an award at your next customer appreciation event. Giving your best referral sources a way to share their success with others, while promoting your business, is a great way to get more customer referrals. Make a big deal about it; make them say "wow" (more on the "wow" in just a moment).

4. Remind your customers. Finally, if you really want referrals, you have to remind people you exist. Studies have found that you have no more than three days of top-of-mind awareness after a positive interaction with a customer and that it is during those three days that customers are most likely to refer. You can increase the chance for customer referrals beyond those 72 hours when you use a newsletter, greeting card, or individual note to create an additional positive interaction.

Now, let's come back to the "wow."

The "wow factor" or "wow experience" plays a HUGE role in earning referrals.

When you deliver a wow experience, you create an experience that stays with your customer. It's something they share with their family, friends, neighbors, and colleagues.

Just consider the words of Warren Buffett:

"Tomorrow morning, when you look in the mirror after you've gotten up, just write — put it in lipstick or whatever you want on the mirror — just put 'delight my customer.'"

Warren Buffett knows business. He is, after all, a genius investor, the CEO of Berkshire Hathaway, and, according to Forbes, worth about $79 billion. So, when Mr. Buffett says the No. 1 way to grow is to do a *great* job delighting customers into naturally giving you referrals, you listen.

Walt Disney, the man who founded a company that became a cultural phenomenon and is known for its incredible customer experience, also has words on the topic: "Do what you do so well that they will want to see it again and bring their friends." Disney was right.

There is a truth all businesses need to take seriously: You can't afford to do a bad job when it comes to customer service.

The odds are already stacked against you. According to The White House Office of Consumer Affairs, a bad experience will reach twice the number of people that a good experience will reach.

Fortunately, referral marketing is so organic that the first steps come naturally when you put in the effort and do a good job. Just start with the basics. Keep your customer satisfaction ratings high by making and keeping basic business promises. *Under promise* and *over deliver*, and when that doesn't happen, apologize and accept responsibility for your mistakes. I bring this up because, let's face it, mistakes will happen. Nobody's perfect.

One of the things we do at The Newsletter Pro after we make a mistake is send what we call a "humble pie": a specific, targeted apology gift that shows our clients we're doing everything we can to listen and respond in spite of our mistakes. It's a small gesture that goes a long way.

"The bottom line is this: Even satisfied customers need encouragement to share."

That all said, just doing a "good" job only goes so far. Research done by Texas Tech pointed out that while 83% of satisfied customers are willing to refer, only 29% will actually do so. The bottom line is this: Even satisfied customers need encouragement to share.

How do you provide that encouragement?

One way to encourage this is by going above and beyond. The dentist's office is rarely anyone's favorite place to be, but with a little bit of "going the extra mile," the dental office experience can become more than just tolerable. It can become enjoyable.

Create an experience that is about everything but the chair or the array of dentist tools. It could be perks in the waiting room, like a spa-like reception area with hot towels and a soothing ambiance. Those perks can extend into the appointment rooms: TVs with streaming content, massage chairs, and so on.

More than in-office perks, just about any business can show their clients how much they care through appreciation events or giveaways. A number of our clients hold yearly appreciation events to do just this. Some also do community appreciation events to target a wider audience. They invite customers, their families, and their friends, whether those people use the business or not.

Some of the events are like mini carnivals, while others are more like sit-down dinners. It all depends on the demographic you serve and what's most meaningful for them. Either way, these experiences give you the opportunity to tap into a wealth of referrals.

But don't forget to leverage your position as "the expert."

Going above and beyond isn't just about the amenities and events. While those are great, you cannot deny the value of *information*. Always position yourself as the expert: the person in your community or industry who knows what they're talking about.

Circling back to the dentist example, as a dentist, you might offer a free report on the "7 Common Reasons People Get Chronic Headaches and Simple Home Remedies to Stop the Pain" or something similar that you know affects a percentage of your patients.

In this report, you would discuss all seven reasons, two of which might be TMJ disorder and teeth grinding. You would then provide solutions and home remedies to relieve the pain as well as suggest they come and see you (or another medical provider, when appropriate) if they are experiencing certain symptoms.

Now, when a friend of your patient is complaining about headaches, your patient can say, "You know, my dentist has this free report on common headache causes and some simple ways to relieve the pain — you should get a copy." How likely do you think their friend is to grab that free report? This person is looking for a solution to their problem, and you've handed it to them on a silver platter.

By this point, the referral has been introduced to the practice and has already received some very useful information that has helped them solve a problem. The person giving the referral has provided assistance to a friend as well as an endorsement for your business. The practice has a new prospect that they know they can follow up with and get in for an appointment. Everyone wins.

This scenario is a great example of how referrals come from providing customers with care and value, instead of simply trying to make a buck. Like Zig Ziglar would say, "If you help enough people get what they want, you'll get what you want."

In our years of running newsletter marketing campaigns, we've learned that doing more than what's required is only the first step toward cultivating referrals. Once you've delighted your customers, it's time to take things a step further by building a valuable referral program.

To sum up, a successful referral program involves ...

1. Delivering a "wow" experience.

2. Encouraging customers to refer others in exchange for potentially earning a reward. One of our clients gives away a big-screen TV every year to the customer who makes the most referrals, while others hold monthly referral contests. There are so many options.

3. Having a system to gather and track those referrals.

Once you've created an effective referral program, stay top of mind with your contacts by using strategic marketing tools, like newsletters, to "delight your customers." You'll be able to maximize not just your customers' experiences, but your profits as well.

ARE YOU DELIGHTING YOUR CUSTOMERS ENOUGH FOR THEM TO RECOMMEND YOU?

Visit **www.stoplosingcustomersbook.com/resources** for follow-up steps to success.

ACTION STEPS TO BUILDING A WINNING REFERRAL PROGRAM:

_____

_____

_____

_____

_____

_____

_____

_____

_____

CHAPTER 6:
HOW TO DEVELOP A BUSINESS MODEL AND COMPANY CULTURE BASED ON RELATIONSHIPS WITH CUSTOMERS

———

I have no doubt a number of your customers do love you, but I also have no doubt churn is still an issue. Complaints don't always correlate to churn.

The main reason for this is that most small businesses simply don't hear about problems ... EVER! Let me ask you this: What do you do when you hear a complaint? Most people simply solve the issue and move on. The problem is that most people don't complain. Only 4% of customers complain when there is an issue, and 91% of those who don't complain will blacklist your company and simply not do business with you again.

There are multiple ways to gauge how much your customers like you and the quality of your customer service. One great way is through the use of a net promoter score (NPS).

NPS is very simple and typically asks a single question: *How likely are you to recommend [brand] to a friend or colleague?*

Use a scale of 1–10, with a score of 1–6 being detractors, 7–8 being passive, and 9–10 being promoters. Your score can range from -100 to +100 points. If you had -100, all your customers basically hate you, and at +100, all of your customers love you. A score of 0 is considered average, where half of your customers are very happy and half of your customers are at risk of leaving. To calculate your score, simply subtract the number of detractors from the number of promoters.

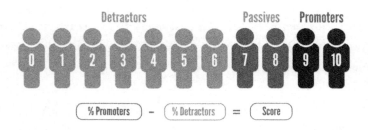

World-class companies like Disney, Costco, and Zappos will have scores of 70+ points. Amazing companies will have a score of 50+ points. Good companies will have a score of 0–49 points. Companies that need improvement will have negative scores.

Once you have your NPS, you'll know where you're starting at and how much work needs to be done, but this will give you a good idea of how your customers feel about your brand.

Improving Your NPS Score

The changes I'll be suggesting throughout this book are all designed to improve your relationship with your customers, prospects, vendors, employees, and so on, and the first part I'm going to discuss is how to get your employees on board.

Another way to determine how well your company treats its customers is by paying very close attention to customer feedback. Every time you get a complaint, you should treat it like gold. This customer, who is being a pain in the neck right now, may be unintentionally informing you of a major issue at your business that is costing you thousands, or even hundreds of thousands, of dollars in the form of lost customers.

If you only listen and solve the complaint for that singular customer, you're missing a huge opportunity to decrease churn across the board.

The Story of "Battle-Ax" Bertha

During my early days in business, when I was the sales department, customer service manager, and head bottle washer, I got a call from a client who was a lawyer. The client called to ask if I knew anything about getting a negative review removed from Google about the firm. I told him I did have a few tactics and shared those with him. During our time on the call, I also looked up the review and read it. Right before the call was about to end, I worked up the nerve to tell him that he may be able to take care of this one review, but that it wouldn't fix his problem, and that there would be more bad reviews to follow. My client obviously didn't like the sound of that and asked me what I was talking about. I told him his front desk person was horrible and should be fired immediately. He was caught off guard and said, "Bertha? Really?"

I told him, without a shadow of a doubt, that his front desk person was costing him an incredible amount in profits. I told him I could market for him until pigs fly, but my efforts would be futile unless he fired her and replaced her with a new person who doesn't suck at their job. Next, I asked a simple question: Do you record calls? The answer was no, so I told him to simply leave his door open or lurk near her desk out of sight a few times while she was on the phone and just listen to how she handled his calls. To my client's credit, he did, and he found that Bertha was awful. She was rude, played Solitaire on the computer while on the phone with clients, and, frankly, could not care less if anyone made an appointment or not. Shortly after our call and his investigation, Battle-Ax Bertha was well-axed. After that, something amazing happened: The firm was instantly busier with more appointments and more new clients. Many of the existing clients actually thanked the lawyer for firing Bertha and then relayed stories of how much they hated working with her. This is all too common.

"The moral of the story is you have to inspect what you expect."

The moral of my story here isn't to fire your front desk person (unless justified). The moral of the story is you have to inspect what you expect. Of course, Battle-Ax Bertha isn't playing Solitaire while you're looking. Of course she treats you well — you cut the check.

Having good employees is crucial to success in the relationship economy, and few companies understand how important a good team is to sales and success better than Zappos. When it started in 1999, Zappos was just a company that sold shoes over the internet — innovative, sure, but not brilliant. The genius came when Tony Hsieh took over as CEO in 2002. He decided that the company should focus on culture and customer experience, not sales. He saw the relationship economy on the horizon! In a bold move, he cut Zappos' drop-ship business and 25% of the company's sales along with it.

People probably thought Tony was crazy, but the risk paid off. Today, Zappos delivers a client experience that a lot of people, including the knowledgeable folks at Forbes, consider pure genius.

The biggest indicator of its success is that the company's clients are insanely loyal: 75% of its sales come from returning customers. That is a big deal in business. In fact, it's such a jaw-dropper that when Glassman Wealth Services CEO Barry Glassman wanted to teach his employees a lesson about customer service, he handed them each $100 and told them to buy two pairs of Zappos shoes (one to keep, and one to return) and report back. Zappos itself claims to be "maniacally obsessed" with customer service.

Here are just a few of the ways Zappos wows its customers:

- It offers a *365-day return policy.*
- Its customers get free shipping *and* free returns.
- Its employees don't believe in phone trees.
- Its employees don't use scripts.
- It has a 24/7 call center.
- It doesn't time-restrict customer calls. (Once, it's rumored, a Zappos rep spent more than *10 hours* on the line with a client.)
- It has been known to refund damaged products and replace them *for free.*
- It encourages employees to go above and beyond.

As nutty as a 365-day return policy might sound, the most dramatic bullet point in that list is actually the last one. When it comes to making customers happy, Zappos employees are not shy; they'll do whatever it takes. Sometimes that means sending flowers to a customer's sick mother. Other times, it means shipping a personalized care package to an American soldier who called from overseas. Employees do all that on Zappos' dime, and yet the company still hit $1 billion in sales in less than 10 years. There's a reason why I encourage my team at The Newsletter Pro to do the same thing. We regularly get emails from customers to thank us for our relationship-building efforts, whether those efforts were delivered in the form of a bouquet of flowers after a death in the family or a bag of a client's favorite taffy, just because. Empowering my people to take those steps has done wonders for our client experience and retention.

As you might have already figured out, the not-so-secret secret behind Zappos' success with customers is that it treats its employees right. Building a happy, close-knit, fun company culture starts on day one. In fact, after two weeks of training, if a new hire isn't happy, Zappos *offers them a $2,000 payout to quit.* Yeah, you read that right. That's how important it is to the company that everyone is 110% on board with its mission and core values.

On top of giving employees the power to handle their customers the way they want to without oversight, Zappos also offers "Zapponians" plenty of team-building exercises, generous perks (from happy hours to an excess of vacation time), and opportunities to grow. It continued those programs even as the company grew, changed hands, and restructured. Tony literally wrote the book on employee culture in 2013. It's called "Delivering Happiness: A Path to Profits, Passion, and Purpose," and if you're smart, you'll go out and get a copy.

So, what can you learn from Zappos' success story? Well, the No. 1 lesson is that the relationship economy is real, and it isn't to be underestimated. The No. 2 lesson is that if you want to build relationships with your clients, you need to start by doing it with your employees. If they don't love you, not one of the clients they work with really will, either.

At The Newsletter Pro, we try to embody some of the same values that Zappos does, but we do it in our own unique way. One of the more recent strategies I've implemented to improve our culture and customer service is our "Around the World" mission. We have a three-year goal to be mailing over 1,000,000 newsletters per month by the end of 2020. We have milestones and check-ins that tell us if we're on pace or off pace toward the goal. At each check-in, there is a prize of some kind for the team. These are pictures from around my office of the mission posters we've created:

To launch the mission, we closed down a few hours early, and I explained to the whole team what the mission was, why it was a good idea, and more importantly, why and how they affect the outcome of the mission. We themed the meeting as if we were on a plane. We had soda and snacks that you'd find in first class of any major airline. We made it more of a pep rally as opposed to a normal boring meeting. Each team member got their pilot's license (a simple laminated card pictured below). Once we complete each leg of the journey, they get another sticker for their pilot's license.

When we hit our goal at the end of 2020, I have one major prize for the whole team ... I'm taking them all to Las Vegas for a long weekend. We're going to party and have good food and celebrate our win as a team.

I put so much effort into making the employee experience great here because it is not enough for just me to be onboard with relationship marketing; I have to get my team on board or move them out. I know that sounds harsh, and I'm not suggesting you don't give people a chance to improve. But we have to learn from stories like Battle-Ax Bertha. If you don't act when someone sucks at their job or doesn't want to grow in the same direction as the company, you will eventually slowly decline until you sell for pennies on the dollar — or even worse, go out of business. If that ends up being your situation, even after learning what you need to do to make that not happen, then I have no sympathy for you.

Don't get confused. The No. 1 asset of any business is its people (your employees). With that said, those same people can be your greatest liabilities as well. That is why you have to be slow to hire and quick to fire. You can't allow someone to rest on their laurels. I'm glad you were a great employee two years ago, but what about today? How is your performance this year, this month, heck, even this week?

Most employees want to do well, most want to learn, and most want their work to have meaning, but not all of them want any of those things. The ones who don't have to go, and they have to go fast, as they are causing irreparable harm to you, your family, the other employees in your office, their families, and your customers.

One of the core values we have at The Newsletter Pro is Deliver a WOW! The employees who are passionate about delivering a wow stay, and the ones who don't prioritize the customer in that way do not. To us, delivering a wow means always finding ways to surprise and delight the customer. Go above and beyond to take care of the customer; share in the good times and the bad times with them. No one has ever been written up or fired at The Newsletter Pro for going above and beyond for a customer ... even though there has been a time or two when someone has gone too far and spent *way* too much, but those instances are rare.

How can you wow your customers? How can you empower your team to wow them?

Customer service is so bad in America that literally just doing little things that are outside the norm or simply bringing a smile to the customers' faces goes a long way.

We like to make our wows random as long as every customer gets wowed randomly once or twice a year at a minimum.

Below are three stories (out of 300-plus examples I have) of times we've wowed clients and the letters or notes we've received after the fact.

> Hi, Shaun.
>
> This is just a quick little note to say ...
>
> My writer is da bomb!
>
> I have lost sleep some nights worrying that I won't be "good enough" to give her enough information to write about.
>
> I have stepped out of important meetings — the latest one at an Inner Circle meeting in Chicago — just to talk to her ... and I felt happy that I did!
>
> At times, I have forgotten that she was going to call. We "winged the interview," and she still made "stone soup" out of our conversation.
>
> I like that she is always in a good mood!
> I like that her interviews always challenge me!
> I like that she always seems prepared!

I like that she is a geek!
I like that she is a cat person!
I like the quality of every article she has written for my newsletter!

Heck, I even like the quality of the other "custom" articles she writes for your general newsletter use! And ... most of all, I like her positive, supportive telephone voice and always bubbly attitude when representing The Newsletter Pro!

Whatever you're paying her is not enough!
(But you don't need to tell her THAT until her next review comes around.)
I really enjoy being a client of The Newsletter Pro, and my writer is one of the main reasons why I do!

—Travis West, Building Air Quality

My project manager sent me the first draft of my first FSI (free-standing insert), which I opened this morning. It literally wowed me.

What I mean is that I was sitting in a coffee shop with my laptop and I said, "wow" loud enough that other customers looked over at me.

This FSI my team created is exactly the format and style that I had in my brain but have never been able to put on paper. I feel proud that this will be going out under my name. Great job!

—Jeremy Wyatt, Harrison Law Group

Each month, my terrific team makes sure I get content together that is right for my readers. They make sure the newsletter looks good and comes on time, and they give me lots of ideas.

In addition, they are given room to be awesome people at work.

Here's what I mean. Recently, Satchmo, my beloved bulldog, died of cancer. I was — and still am — heartbroken.

Since Satchmo had written a cover article for the newsletter this year, I shared with the team the eulogy I wrote for him.

In response, they sent my family a beautiful memorial tribute to Satchmo, complete with a quote that made me cry and one of my favorite photos of him.

They just sent it, along with a sweet note. I've met Shaun and heard him speak often enough to know that this beautiful and heartfelt gift did not require three layers of management approval to be sent.

This now hangs in my home, and every time I see it, I remember their kindness.

—Francine Love, Love Law Firm

Can you imagine how different your business could be if you added a little wow factor? Oftentimes, I think entrepreneurs forget that we are all in the people business. Our job is to serve our customers and our employees. If we do that, we get to keep our jobs and, with any luck, make some money as well. The best part is that wowing customers doesn't have to be expensive. As you can see from the first message, that writer is simply good at their job. The cost for the company was hiring correctly and good training. The project manager was just doing their job, but they did it with care and concern for the project. We have systems and processes in place to give us the best chance to hit the mark each time. Do we always literally make people say "wow" out loud in the coffee shop? I'm going to guess we don't, but with the correct systems in place and amazing people, we have a shot. I'm sure there was some cost associated with the final experience, but I have no idea what it was because Francine is correct. It didn't take any management layers to approve that gift. The team has a budget, and they simply submitted the request for purchase from their budget, and one of my team members ordered the gift. It is important that you give your team room to deliver the wow.

However, the easiest way to guarantee your team never goes above and beyond is to chastise them or make them feel foolish when they do go above and beyond. I've actually witnessed this at companies where an employee does something nice for a customer, and they get a verbal tongue-lashing for the free thing they gave away. That employee will never put their neck out on the line to help someone like that again out of fear.

All that said, if you don't have all your employees on board with working for the customer and consistently delivering a wow for the customer, you can end up like Victoria's Secret, who only focused on ROI.

Case Study: How One Mega Company Lost $10 Billion by Being Penny-Wise and Pound-Foolish and What You Can Learn From Their Mistakes

In February 2016, L Brands, the parent company of Victoria's Secret, fired star CEO Sharen Turney and hired a new CEO, Stuart Burgdoerfer, who decided to take a fresh look at the company. Burgdoerfer started off by asking this question: If they started Victoria's Secret in 2016, how would they go about marketing and selling? On the surface, this seems like a fair question, but there is one big problem: The answer is irrelevant. They didn't start the brand in 2016, and the way you build a startup is different than the way you build a multibillion-dollar company. If they were starting in 2016, they'd likely be online only, at least to start.

With this faulty question at hand, the executive team at Victoria's Secret decided to make a huge change to their marketing plan and save $150 million per year by cutting their much-beloved catalog and discontinue their swimwear line, despite it having $500 million in sales.

At the time, one Twitter user commented on the news that Victoria's Secret had discontinued their catalog by saying, "In big news, the Victoria's Secret catalog has been discontinued. 'We have the internet, we don't need it anymore,' said 13-year-old boys."

I would expect nothing less from the internet and even those in the marketing community as a whole. The gross misunderstanding of how marketing works today, especially by the media, is a huge part of the issue. All most of these folks know is what they read on Inc. or Business Insider. They see headlines daily about the death of anything that isn't Twitter, Facebook, and Snapchat. Although, now the death of Twitter is a regular story as well. They don't understand that those catalogs were driving millions in sales.

If we go back to the cutting of swimwear, the executives' reason for cutting swimwear was that the sales growth was flat in Q1 of 2016. The category had grown 10% in Q1 of 2015 but one bad year-over-year growth period and I guess you cut a half-billion-dollar category. Is it possible they just missed the trends for 2016 and needed to replace some fashion designers? Could it have been that they weren't marketing enough and that's why sales were flat? I guess we'll never know because these executives decided no one would miss half a billion dollars in sales.
I don't know who else they have on the executive team, but they should fire them all after this round of decision making.

I first wrote about the cutting of the catalog shortly after it was making the rounds on the business news sites. I felt it was a dumb decision; this catalog was driving people online and into the stores. Privately to some of my friends, we talked about the massive hit the stock price was going to take and how it may make sense to short the stock, which was ultimately a good investment.

About 16 months after the executive team at Victoria's Secret made those calls, it was clear how things had played out. On April 1, 2016, the stock price for L Brands was $88.08. On Sept. 1, 2017, the stock price was $37.46, and sales were down by 20%. Not surprisingly, 6% of the decrease came from the discontinued swimwear line. The other 14% ... maybe the discontinued catalog. These yahoos saved $150 million in advertising costs, likely gave themselves a bonus for doing it, and cut the stock price by 67.5%, erasing roughly $15 billion in market cap — 100x times what they saved in advertising costs.

Victoria's Secret is still struggling as we get deeper into 2019. In February, the brand announced it would close 53 stores across the country, citing a "decline in performance" and a poor holiday quarter. In May, Business Insider reported the company was in "ongoing collapse" (surprise!). Some people blame the brand's failure to market inclusively, while others point to the bad rap it earned during the #MeToo movement. Personally, I think it all leads back to 2016. And because the executive team just doesn't learn from past mistakes, L Brands confirmed in May that it has canceled the annual Victoria's Secret Fashion Show, probably because it dropped down to 3.3 million viewers last year. Now, it will lose all of the people who bothered to stick around too!

On the surface, we all do what these executives do. We want everything to work perfectly and fall perfectly and neatly into a fully trackable and calculable ROI. Well, good luck with that, because it is not the world we live in for most media and most products. The catalog has been shown time and time again to be difficult to track but has a massive effect on the bottom line. Why? Because people get the catalog, browse it, and go to the website or store. Catalogs are so effective that there are online-only companies that mail them out. Bodenusa.com and Bonobos.com are two online-only retailers that mail catalogs. In the age of online ordering and the death of retail, all shopping is going to be done on your phone starting any day now, so why would anyone in the online space wade into the nasty and dirty area of catalog sales? The only logical guess is they are making money. It's hard to track the catalog and its direct sales, but what is not hard to track is an increase in sales.

This brings me back to the start of this rant, which is that you cannot track 100% ROI any longer if you have any complications in your business. And if you don't have complications in your business, you have a very, very small, simple business that is not thriving in the relationship economy.

But what happens when you have a complicated business or tons of competition? What happens when you are a service provider like a dentist, lawyer, physical therapist, or HVAC technician and there are hundreds of competitors in your area? You don't have a simple business now.

You may be thinking, "But Shaun, I can totally track 100% ROI. We do it in my business all the time, and we're a big business!" That is because you're tracking first touch or last touch, not 100% direct ROI. So, if you track first touch and the lead comes in from Facebook and after eight months of getting emails and direct mail, seeing you at a trade show, and reading your newsletter, the lead finally purchases with first touch, you give the credit for the sale to Facebook. With last touch, the credit goes to the trade show or a phone call after the trade show. Neither of these is even close to being correct. It took dozens of touches for someone to become your customer.

Now, you may be saying, "Shaun, I don't do lead generation or collect data until they become a customer, so my tracking works." Well, we need to talk about not doing any lead generation another time, but I do know that is common in a number of businesses that think that's just how it is done in their industry, but you're just being naive now. All the research shows that people need to be exposed to you at least eight times on average before they even know you exist, which means they saw you in another way, shape, or form numerous times that you couldn't track.

It is this same bad logic and basic misunderstanding of how marketing works that caused the executives at Victoria's Secret to cancel their catalogs and lose billions.

I get this on the newsletter side all the time. Prospects misunderstand the purpose of a newsletter and want to try and turn it into some lead generation piece, which 9 out of 10 times is a bad idea. The goal of the newsletter isn't typically to get people who have never heard of you before to read it cold. To make that work, you better have some damn good stuff to say and some amazing offers.

IKEA and Costco both send out a catalog — Costco's is more of half-catalog, half-newsletter, but that's not the point. In 2016, IKEA sent 213 million catalogs. In 2013, Costco sent over 103 million catalogs. They can't track those 100%, that's for sure. Can you imagine what it costs to send 213 million IKEA catalogs? It has to be nearly $2 per catalog minimum.

Hopefully, I've educated and entertained you enough to get to this point in the book because all the examples and all the facts have built up to one word: Stop!

"You are hurting your own growth by not realizing that so much of your marketing is interconnected."

You are shooting yourself in the foot by trying to track 100% ROI on every transaction. You are hurting your own growth by not realizing that so much of your marketing is interconnected. Your newsletter is connected to the emails you send and the reviews you have online. Facebook ads are connected to your website or landing page and the emails you send or the lead magnet you gave them to opt in. The sign on the road that people pass by every day is connected to the postcards and direct mail pieces you send out and the phone calls you make. The person who answers your phones and makes appointments is connected to all the marketing. It is all connected.

This creates another problem though: What should *you* do? You can't do all marketing.

The answer is simple. You need to do the fundamentals. First, determine what the goal of the marketing is. Is it lead generation, nurture, customer service, upsells, retention, referral, or all of the above?

Next, work on the foundational pieces: answering the phone, customer service, nurture, retention, referrals. The marketing that you need for this is typically phone and customer service training as well as email and newsletter marketing.

Finally, you need a system to ask, reward, and communicate about referrals. You have to get this stuff right before you even think about more leads. This is the backbone. You want to track individual performances (on the phone and in customer service) and the campaigns (based on if we got referrals or not), but you are not trying to track any of the media specifically because it is not lead generation. If your emails aren't getting a response, maybe they are boring. If your referral program isn't working, you're likely being too cheap. Give a better gift, create a better experience, you get the point. These are foundational parts of campaigns.

Once you have those few things on point, then you can move on to lead generation. This is where we can get much more accurate on the tracking because we are asking it to bring in new leads. What you want to do here is track all the steps in the campaign, from lead generation to conversion. For example, if you generate the lead on Facebook, to convert that lead, you need to send emails and make phone calls; Facebook is only one component. You may be getting amazing leads on Facebook, but the person making the phone calls sucks. That is the real reason your Facebook campaign isn't working, but you don't look at it from the campaign standpoint; you've only been looking at it by lead source and making decisions with bad data.

At the end of the day, this is work, so you'll have a hard time outsourcing it. It sucks, but this is the work that changes lives, most notably yours and your family's lives. This is work worth doing and doing right. This is worth rereading and making sure you understand the details of what I wrote here, because I can assure you that your competitors don't understand what you and I have just gone over, which will allow you to stay ahead of them and even crush them if you so desire.

I'll close with this thought: What is your company's most valuable asset? It's your customer and prospect database. Communicating with them — be it through catalog, newsletter, or smoke signals, and providing them value, reminding them who you are, what you do, and that you're still in business — is the most profitable thing you can do. Don't forget: It is far easier to sell an existing customer something else than it is to find a new customer.

Don't make the mistake that Victoria's Secret did and assume that an item that is hard to track, like a catalog or print newsletter or most relationship marketing pieces, isn't making you money. Don't assume that everything is going digital because it is not, not even close. Be smarter than that. Don't be penny-wise and pound-foolish. Be smart about your tracking; invest in your foundation areas first, and you will crush it.

DO YOU GIVE A DAMN
ABOUT YOUR EMPLOYEES?

Visit **www.stoplosingcustomersbook.com/resources**
for follow-up steps to success.

ACTION STEPS TO GIVE MORE DAMNS:

_____

_____

_____

_____

_____

_____

_____

_____

_____

_____

CHAPTER 7:
HOW TO MAKE A SUCCESSFUL MARKETING CAMPAIGN

—

Below is an action plan for you to use to maximize what you've learned to this point. Don't just skip to this chapter, though. To become a successful relationship marketer, you can't cut corners. Your passion for your customers' experience must be your primary focus, and you won't be able to develop an unparalleled customer relationship without all the information in this book.

How to Decrease Churn and Increase Profits

When you're crafting your strategy, you need to first consider two things: Who is your average customer, and who is your ideal customer? The reason you look at your current average and ideal customers is that your average may not be who you really want. When you don't have a plan for who you're targeting, you just get who comes. The problem is the person who comes may be a PITA, broke, or just plain difficult. Since we still have to work with the current client, you need to know who they are, but we need to start to shift our marketing to make sure we're attracting the ideal client for us.

For example, if your average customer is a mom between the ages of 35 and 45 and has kids in the house, you'll have very different messaging than if your average customer is an empty-nester between 55 and 65 years old. Their season of life is different, and in turn, your copy, content, selection, and messaging will reflect those different seasons. That's why you have to know who you're targeting. If you've been attracting Mom and really should have been targeting Grandma, you're likely hating sales life because you keep dealing with people who aren't as likely to buy.

It is very important that you focus on the type of content your target demographic wants to consume, regardless of your thoughts on the value of that content.

"Who cares what I like? I'm not my customer."

As an example, I'm not into the celebrity gossip content, but if my target demographic loves it, that's what I'd talk about. Thankfully for my sanity, that's not the case. It wouldn't matter that I didn't like that topic or type of content if that is what my client wants to read about. Who cares what I like? I'm not my customer. Once I know what my customer wants from a content standpoint, I'm going to figure out how to tie my marketing and copy to that type of content. By doing this, I will be speaking the language of my ideal prospect and will not only get more ideal prospects in my front door but I will also be more clear on where I advertise to get those customers.

Once you know your demographic and understand how you need to communicate with your ideal prospects and customers about topics they care about, then it's time to look at the tactical pieces of communication, how to use them, and even why it makes sense to use them.

The first piece of media is a must-have, and it's something I consider to be the foundation of an amazing marketing strategy.

1.   **Print Newsletter:** A print newsletter is the foundation of your marketing campaign for a variety of reasons. A good print newsletter should be personal. The cover should have an article written by you (or ghostwritten) that lets people look behind the curtain to see the wizard. It also should have useful content for your end-user that has little or nothing to do with your business and can include up to one page worth of content about your business, products, or services. A print newsletter is a must for any relationship marketer, regardless of who creates it. Just do it so you can see the results.

There are a few reasons a print newsletter is first on the list.

Newsletters have a near 100% deliverability rate. One of the biggest issues with email and social media is the abysmal deliverability and consumption rates. The average email open rate is about 10% currently, and the average organic Facebook reach is less than 1%. You can't build a relationship with anyone if they don't know you're communicating with them.

We're also going to use some of the content from our newsletter in other marketing. I'll point out when and where to do that.

Another reason we start with newsletters is it allows us to live in the customers' space. What I mean by that is the average newsletter has an in-home or office shelf life of four months before it is tossed out. That can add up to a ton of impressions over time.

The newsletter is also a place where we can ensure our marketing message gets out to both clients and prospects. We can even segment the message so clients get one message and prospects get another. The newsletter gives us media we own, which allows us to use this relationship piece to promote our specials, experiences, and referral contests with the whole list with minimal additional investment in marketing dollars.

2. **Your Blog/Website:** I may not have gone into the SEO business, but I know enough about SEO to know you need to have regular content posted to your blog to stay in the good graces of the almighty Google. One of the easiest places to get good, unique, fresh content is from the articles in your monthly newsletter. Take each article that is unique to you and relevant to prospects, have some basic onsite SEO done to these articles, then post them on your blog. This will allow you to have regular content without additional investment of marketing dollars.

3. **Weekly Reading Emails:** Each week, you should send an email with a good opening paragraph from you (think 100–250 words) and a few pieces of content that your ideal customer would find interesting. At The Newsletter Pro, we make the interesting piece of content each week an article from our blog.

4. **Birthday Cards:** It doesn't get more personal than someone's birthday, and a simple but effective way to build a relationship with someone is to acknowledge their birthday and possibly even get them a gift. If you're a local business, the gift I prefer is a free birthday dinner.

Here's a birthday card copy example: **Come in anytime in the month of October and enjoy a free meal on us up to a value of $12.99.**

This no-strings-attached gift certificate is a welcome treat and is a great marketing tool for the restaurant. One word of warning: Don't let a restaurant try and put lame restrictions on the gift certificate. Most people don't eat alone on their birthday, so making it buy one, get one free or 1/2 off any meal makes you look lame. It would be better to just say happy birthday. If you can't or don't want to find a restaurant to comp the free meal, then either just say happy birthday or buy a $5 Starbucks or Cold Stone Creamery gift card and send those instead.

> **5. Gifting:** A killer relationship strategy is gift-giving. Some people use this strategy for Christmas or an anniversary, but I prefer the gift-giving to be random. I want the customer to be delighted and surprised, but that won't happen if they're getting tons of gifts from a variety of people at the same time. Now, some professions can't give out gifts over $10 or $25 dollars ... some annual customer values don't justify gifts greater than the above dollar amounts. I have good news though: There are a ton of ways to give gifts even when you can't spend a lot of money.

One of the single easiest gifts to give is information. There are two primary types of info. One type would be something like this book. You could send 100 or 1,000 books out to clients over the course of a year with a note that thanks them and maybe even asks for a referral.

You could also create a small product that helps improve your customers' lives. As an example, last year, I sent each of my clients a gift based on something I called "The S**t I Don't Want to Do Strategy." I know, it's a classy name. Basically, we sent them a framed, one-page worksheet that had a list where they write down all the activities don't want to be doing and shouldn't be wasting time on. For example, until just four years ago, I was the person who went to the post office every day to drop off the mail. That was not a smart use of my time even four years ago. I included a little instruction book on how to use the worksheet and a reason why I thought this gift would be better than any other simple item I could have gotten them. The gift was a huge hit and is a simple way to solve any industry rules that won't allow you to do gift-giving.

One thing to keep in mind is that people don't like to feel they owe you one. So, shortly after any gift, you need to give the customer who got the gift the chance to reciprocate by sending them some marketing that has an offer for them to buy a product or service, or, better yet, a request for a referral. This gives the customer the opportunity to do something nice for you so they don't feel like the relationship is one-sided.

6. Experience Marketing: Developing a plan to create unique experiences for customers and prospects is also an incredibly effective tool for building relationships with prospects and clients. Face-to-face time with customers and prospects is invaluable. Recently, we've started putting on two-day trainings at my office where I go over a slew of marketing strategies and tactics for those looking to scale up and grow their business. The impact has been amazing. Since we rarely see customers face-to-face, this has allowed us to deepen our relationship with the customers who attend, and the prospects get to meet us and see how we operate before they make a buying decision. We're currently planning on holding these bootcamps at least quarterly. If you want to check them out to mimic or simply attend, go to www.newsletterpro.com/scaleup to get more info.

Another type of experience-based marketing is the customer appreciation event. I've seen these done where a company rents out a movie theater and gets popcorn and soda for everyone. I've also seen it done in a park where a company rents the park and puts on a family-friendly event and uses the time as both a customer appreciation and referral event. To turn it into a referral event, they ask each customer to bring a family member, friend, or neighbor. When you register to get a wrist band to play on the bounce houses or get your face painted, the company is able to find out if you're a current customer or referral. Referrals get different colored bands and are given an onsite special offer to book an appointment or make a purchase at the event.

The promotion of this event should happen in a variety of ways. First, you should talk about it during the months leading up to the event in the newsletter, with the last one or two months including an FSI (free-standing insert) directly pitching the event. After the event, you need to spend two newsletters talking about how amazing the event was and showing pictures so you increase attendance at the next event. You should also do a direct mail campaign to all customers inviting them and follow up with email and even text messaging if you have the ability. Of course, promoting the event on social media is a great idea as well.

> **7. New Customer Experience:** We talked earlier about how dentists lose 6 out of every 10 new patients who walk in the door for the first time. By focusing on the new customer experience, you can greatly increase the number of new customers who become

loyal. This includes a one-time welcome gift bag with a branded water bottle and a T-shirt as well as some useful information. One of the best pieces of useful information is a newsletter or article that tells your origin story. This allows the new customer to start building a bond with you earlier and improves the relationship.

If they are coming into a physical location, we suggest you do a tour of the office. You want to make sure this is choreographed and that you have specific stops that show important company or personal history that can aid you in building a bond with these new customers. As an example, one of my clients served in the U.S. Army, and he has his flag in a frame on a shelf with a picture of his time in the service. When you get the office tour, you stop by that area, and the employee notes that this doctor served our country. Think about how even just that one stop and personal bit of information about the doctor can have a profound impact on retention. Personally, I'm very patriotic. As a kid, I lived on an Air Force base much of my life. My dad spent 29 years with the Air Force, and it means something to me that this doctor is a veteran and served our country. All things being equal, I'd prefer to support the veteran-owned business. Others may not have the same response as I do, but few, if any, would have a negative response to this doctor's military service. If anyone did, you may not want them as a customer anyway.

8. Personal Notes: One tactic we like to employ is this: When we see an article or another piece of content we think our customer would get value out of, we literally send them the content via USPS with a note on it that says, "Thought you'd like this" or "Thought you'd find this interesting –Shaun." These personal touches are so uncommon that they get people talking in a good way about your business. One issue I hear about this tactic is that people don't feel that it is scalable. The reality is that this tactic is easily scalable. Most of your ideal customers are going to be into the same type of content, so finding a handful of good pieces of content that go out to everyone on the list a few times per year isn't that difficult. Of course, if you come across an item for a particular group of customers, by all means, send that, but by and large, you can simply send the majority of your list the same piece.

9. Birthday Lunch: We talked earlier about the birthday card strategy where you buy the customer their birthday dinner, but with local clients, you can take them all (customers whose birthdays fall in that month) to lunch and get some new customers to boot. Here is how it works. Have your team invite every customer who has a birthday in the upcoming month to a free lunch. Tell the customer you want to treat them and two of their friends to lunch to celebrate their birthday. On the day of the lunch, you'll have dozens of customers and their friends show up to eat. Treat everyone to a fixed menu meal, and, of course, spend a bit of time talking with each person at the event. After the event is over, you can give the birthday customers a card. Then you can give another card to each guest that has an offer in it for them to become new customers because they're friends with the birthday customer.

How long would it take using the above tactic to see some serious new customer growth if you did that each month for a year? How much do you think a birthday lunch like this decreases churn? If social media was used properly with pictures, do you think you may be able to get some additional referrals from that? Seems like a no-brainer that you would.

10. Check-In Call: One of the positions at my company is the customer success manager. This position has three primary purposes:

1. To help clients if they need strategy help, advice, or have an issue.
2. To check in on clients and make sure they're happy and receiving the value they want/need from our products, services, and employees.
3. To upsell where appropriate.

The customer success manager knows these simple check-in calls are always appreciated, even when they're short. No one wants to feel like a number or that you're indifferent to them, so put a little soul back into your marketing and reach out to check on your customers. It will be very appreciated and can lead to referrals or additional sales opportunities and allow you to get in front of an issue that may cause churn if left unchecked.

11. Short Personalized Videos: We all are walking around with a video camera in our pockets, and we rarely use it for relationship building or marketing. Think about how powerful it would be to send off personalized messages to each customer via a short video, thanking them for a purchase or for a first-time visit and inviting them back.

Let's imagine a scenario: You go into a law firm for a consultation meeting with a lawyer. You get the office tour, and you're learning more about the firm's origin story, the same one you read about in the literature you got from them. After the meeting, you get a text from the firm that contains a video of the lawyer calling you by name and letting you know they are there for you to answer any questions. The video concludes by thanking you for coming in and that it was a pleasure to meet you.

You went on tours with other firms, but no one sent you a video at the end of the day. If your experience was equal in every other way, which firm are you going with? The answer seems clear to me: You're going with the one that sent you a personal message in a video.

Here is another spin on this idea: What if you recorded a message for every new client you get, welcoming them to the family? You could make it short but sweet, call them by name, acknowledge them, and let them know you're there for them if they need anything. Wouldn't that alone help at least move the needle a little on new customer churn? Of course it would, because it is so far out of the norm from what we're used to. The automatic assumption would be that this place is different and better.

On top of the above relationship-building and experience-based strategies, you can also use actual sales emails, direct mail pieces, phone calls, and social media posts. By first starting with relationships and then adding in the sales pieces, you take the business from being narcissistic to a well-rounded member of society.

Now, I know I'll have more than a few people who will read this book and think, "I don't need to do any of this. My customers love me!"

My question for you is this: Are you sure?

According to a Bain & Company survey, a full 80% of companies say they deliver superior customer service. My guess is that you feel similarly about your company. The problem is the entrepreneur's thoughts on how they're doing and the customers' thoughts and feelings don't always match up. You see, when Bain & Company surveyed the customers of those same companies, the customers said only 8% of the companies provide superior customer service. Literally one-tenth of customers felt the same way the entrepreneur did.

No relationship grows and thrives on a lack of communication and self-absorbed behaviors. Your company is no different. Don't fool yourself into thinking you're the exception and not the rule. You need this as much as everyone else does. Are you truly committed to growth and change in a positive way? Or do you prefer to do it the way you've always done it and die a slow death the moment anyone with any relationship marketing skills enters your market (assuming they aren't quietly kicking your butt right now)?

On occasion, I will have people ask me *how long* they need to do all this relationship marketing, and my answer is always this: as long as you still want a good growing business with low churn and lots of referrals.

The funny thing about the question is everyone who asks already knows the answer. If you're ever trying to figure out right from wrong in relationship marketing, simply think about courting your spouse or significant other. You wouldn't get them a birthday gift in year one and then in year two tell them to be grateful for what they got last year. It works the same way with customers. When you start this type of business model, you have to continue being in the relationship game as long as you're in business.

DO YOU OWN
YOUR MEDIA?

Visit **www.stoplosingcustomersbook.com/resources**
for follow-up steps to success.

ACTION STEPS TO TELL YOUR STORY THROUGH
MEDIA YOU OWN:

_____

_____

_____

_____

_____

_____

_____

_____

_____

_____

CHAPTER 8:
RELATIONSHIP MARKETING CAMPAIGN DO'S AND DON'TS

—

Don't skip over this section. This is where you round out your action plan and get results from what you're learning.

Now, pick one item from the list below as the next step you'll implement after getting your churn number and starting the newsletter. I've left the blog content and weekend reading off the list, as nearly all of those systems will be taken care of with the content from the newsletter.

Pick one item from this list:

- Birthday Cards
- Gifting
- Experience-Based Marketing
- New Customer Experience
- Birthday Lunch
- Check-in Call
- Short Personalized Videos

Once you have your churn numbers figured out, the newsletter in place, your version of a weekend reading going out, and your website constantly updated with fresh content on a regular basis, you can take a minute to congratulate yourself. You've now taken the first steps toward being a relationship marketer, reducing churn, increasing profits, and building a foundation for your business that will help you grow. And now, we'll dive right into the three rules no business can break if they truly want to grow and thrive.

The 3 'Do Not Break' Rules for Any Business

As mentioned in the previous chapter, we can't expect to make every communication about the business's wants, needs, and desires and still have customers care about.

There are three very important "do not break" rules that you must pay attention to when developing your relationship-marketing communication strategy. As we go through this process and you develop your own action plan, make sure you follow these three rules.

Rule 1: Don't be a narcissist. Your whole communication strategy can't be about your wants, needs, and desires.

Rule 2: Don't be boring. I can't stress this enough. Stop sending out industry garbage. No one wants to know from their dry cleaner what an invisible stain is, nor do they want to see disgusting before-and-after pictures of people who haven't brushed their teeth in a decade.

Rule 3: Communicate often. You have to communicate at a minimum of twice per month with all customers, but weekly is preferred, and in many cases, multiple times per week is justified and necessary.

I can hear the moans and groans from here: "My customers don't want to hear from me that often." That is because you're breaking Rules 1 and 2 and simply don't have a relationship with your customers. Good news, though. We're going to change that by the time you're done implementing the strategies in this book.

Now we're going to dive deep into communication strategies because it can be a place where many people get stuck.

Here are six points you need to take into consideration when developing your company's communication strategy.

1. Frequency of Communication

How often is *too* often to communicate with customers and prospects? This is a great question. So far, I've asked you to communicate a ton! If the thought hasn't come to mind yet, I promise the question was coming. Having the wrong communication strategy can easily cost you money. With too much communication, people opt out and stop paying attention. With too little communication, you miss out on sales because your competition got to them before you did. Or worse, an existing customer leaves and goes to a competitor because they feel you're indifferent to them.

It is far more common that people communicate too little as compared to too much.

Remember earlier when we talked about the fact that 68% of customers leave because they feel you're indifferent to them? Part of that is a lack of communication.

The issue with communication isn't so much how much you're communicating but *what* you communicate. Remember Rule 2 from earlier: Don't be boring.

For example, have you ever taken a long trip with someone and just talked the whole time? You went from one conversation to the next effortlessly and time flew by?

Have you ever been on a long road trip with the kids and nearly every question was "Are we there yet?" and you were constantly breaking up fights?

What you say is what matters when it comes to content, as long as what you say is interesting and relevant to the person you're saying it to.

I want you to think about the personal relationships you have — maybe some of those close friends from high school or college. Of all of these "close" friends, how many are you still close with? How many do you talk with daily, weekly, or even monthly? How many do you only see on Facebook or other social media?

What about your family? Do you speak with your spouse or other loved ones daily? How do the relationships you have with people differ when you speak with them on a regular basis as opposed to quarterly or annually?

Outside of business, those people you speak to often are the people you have the closest relationships with, and those friends from the past are just people you are familiar with or share a history with now.

A few years ago, I was at an event and ran into Christopher Judge. He is an actor, best known for his role in the TV series "Stargate." We got to chatting and ended up hanging out in the bar that evening. Somehow we ended up on the conversation of divorce in Hollywood, and he said, "You know, most people think the reason the divorce rate in Hollywood is so high is because we are all self-absorbed, but in reality, it is because we spend so much time away from our families to film these TV shows or movies that eventually, we just grow apart."

The same can be said for any relationship, including the relationship you have with your clients or customers. The longer you go between communications, the weaker your relationships are with your customers, and the more open they are to using another service or simply forgetting about you altogether. Another wrinkle in this is the type of communication you deliver. If every interaction you have with someone is you asking them for money (i.e., pay your bill, buy my stuff), you're killing the relationship.

We have a saying at The Newsletter Pro: Don't be that guy. Basically, that means none of us ever wants to be the person who doesn't add any value and only pitches. Of course, you can go too far on this spectrum and never pitch, which isn't good either.

Even with the above statement being true, there is still one issue. People want an answer to the question of how much content you can send every day, week, or month without annoying people.

Here are my rules of thumb for sending content.

For email, you can typically send messages daily, with the occasional multiple emails in a single day if you're promoting an event, like a webinar. You may have three emails in a day talking about the webinar, announcing the start of the webinar, and sending out a replay link.

Many people feel daily is too much. I'll often hear "I'd unsubscribe if someone sent me daily emails," but it doesn't matter what *you* would do; it only matters what your customers and prospects would do.

If you are sending useful and entertaining information, people will pay attention.

The same goes for all types of media. Make boring social media posts and you can post as often as you'd like, but no one will care.

For direct mail, you can send as often as your budget allows. The same basic rules apply to direct mail as they do with email. If you send stuff that is dull and not useful, you won't get a response.

The other day, I got a postcard in the mail from a company that asked a question: What do these three things have in common with the organization that sent this postcard? When I flipped over the postcard to find out, it said to stay tuned until XYZ date ... What? Why would I want to eagerly await the answer to this question? Send me a postcard and make one single offer; it's just that simple.

It's this kind of marketing that gives any media a bad name.

You could send a similar postcard like that daily and never get a good enough response to justify the ad spend.

Social media posts should be made often and should be as interesting, relevant, and shareable as possible.

If you want a simpler answer to the question of how often is too often to communicate with prospects and clients, I'll leave you with this thought. Nearly every company I look at, whether that is to buy, to invest in, or as a mastermind member, none of them are overcommunicating. In fact, 100% of them are under-communicating, and most of them are not communicating at all.

This means you can increase what you're sending with little fear that it is going to bite you in the rear.

However, here's one more warning: Any time you increase the volume of communication, you will see additional people tune you out or even unsubscribe from your list. That is okay because it is highly unlikely those were the engaged prospects.

2. Consistency of Communication

The last message I'd ever want to send to customers and prospects is that I'm not consistent or organized. Can you imagine that ad? "Very skilled but unorganized lawyer will fight for your rights. Our lawyer is super inconsistent, but if you get him on a day when he is hot, you'll surely be walking home scot-free. If you happen to get him on an off day, you're looking at 10–20 years for that shoplifting charge." That would be an outrageous ad, and no one would ever publish that and expect results.

Remember earlier when I said actions speak louder than words? It does in your communication as well.

When you take on the task of a regularly scheduled publication and you do not send it out on time, at a minimum, you are telling your customers you are disorganized. Is that the message you want to put out to customers and prospects? No, of course not, because being inconsistent hurts sales, referrals, and retention. If you're not in it for the long haul, don't start. You'll ultimately do more harm than good.

3. Creativity in Your Communication

This step is difficult for many business owners. The primary reason people fail at this is because they simply get busy.

As a fellow business owner, I know how crazy life and business can be. But even when I'm busy, that doesn't give me an excuse to be lazy and boring in my communication with customers and prospects.

As my grandma once told me, paraphrasing Albert Einstein, "The definition of insanity is doing the same thing over and over again when it doesn't work." So, if you keep doing what you're doing now, you'll be in the same place next year.

I have watched countless business owners start down the right path of being creative and useful to their customers, only to self-sabotage and go back to old habits of being the same as everyone else in their industry, which equals boring.

When you're speaking to your ideal reader, you need to communicate information in a way that is interesting, personal, and relevant.

If you head over to my blog (NewsletterPro.com/blog) or read the newsletter I write, you'll notice most of my content is not for people who are new to business. It's not that I don't want to help them — I love starting new businesses and working through those challenges — but most of my products aren't designed for newbies. I don't want to write articles that attract people with 36-person lists. That would be a waste of my time and theirs, as I can't help those people. I write to attract, educate, and entertain entrepreneurs who have real businesses with real business issues.

In my newsletter and blog content, I open up and get personal. People want to do business with people they know, like, and trust ... It is your job to let them know you through quality, creative content, so they have the opportunity to like you and connect with you, which encourages them to trust you.

4. Various Styles of Communication

This one seems like a no-brainer, but so many people mess this up. You cannot have a single method of communicating. Not only is it very unstable (as you never know when a form of communication may become less effective), it also just isn't smart. Think of fax blasts from the '90s; they're now all illegal. People consume information in multiple ways and value types of media differently. It would be much simpler if all communication came via email, but "simple" doesn't mean correct, smart, or profitable. Email deliverability and open rates decline each and every year, which is why so many people are sending even more email — to compensate for the lack of results.

Don't misunderstand me; I am not against email marketing. I am against it being the *only* form of communication. To build a relationship, you should communicate through multiple different media: text, direct mail, smoke signals, etc.

5. Personality and Celebrity

A few years ago, the MGM Grand in Las Vegas ripped out its highly profitable $2 million-a-year but run-of-the-mill restaurant and replaced it with a restaurant created by celebrity chef Michael Mina called Nobhill Tavern. They have since literally tripled sales to $6 million annually. What makes Nobhill Tavern three times better? Is it possible the food being served is 300% better than before? I doubt it.

The addition of celebrity allowed the MGM Grand to increase prices at Nobhill and allowed them to fill the restaurant each night, which was not happening previously. Adding celebrity to restaurants has been a game-changer. Adding celebrity (even local celebrity) or at least personality to any business will be effective because as a society, we're programmed to value personality.

"The point here is that you are in the media."

As I said earlier, people want to do business with people they know, like, and trust, and they're willing to spend more with someone who has personality or celebrity because of how they feel about that person. How can you become the local celebrity in your industry, town, or even state? Some examples of ways to be the celebrity include getting booked on local media, like radio or TV. You can write a book or have one ghostwritten. You can do interviews for magazines or newspapers in your area. You can throw a massive party and invite everyone who fits your customer avatar and get press coverage. The point here is that you are in the media. Some of the media is owned by others (e.g. TV or radio stations), but you can own media. You can have a print newsletter, write a book, or create a local magazine.

6. Quality

The look and feel of your product, service, and marketing matters. You can't claim to be high end and send out items that were last updated in 1990, when New Kids on the Block was a big deal and "Beverly Hills 90210" was a popular TV show.

Your content also can't suck. If it looks like your articles were written by high school freshmen, you're shooting yourself in the foot. When I read articles written by my team, I am always looking for the one (or more) big idea. Why was this piece of content not a waste of time? How did it help the person consuming it? These are two questions you need to ask when you create content.

You can build all the relationships in the world, but if you don't have quality, nothing can help you. If you get many complaints from a quality standpoint, fix that issue first. Once you have a good quality product, it is much easier to build those relationships. After all, if you talk a big game and provide crap, people will feel cheated, and any relationship credibility you've built will evaporate.

Once you've outlined an action plan to develop your relationship marketing strategy to nurture your clients based on the information in this book, then you can move on to building a relationship-marketing strategy for leads and prospects.

ARE YOU A MARKETING "DON'T"? WHICH OF MY "DO NOT BREAK" RULES ARE YOU BREAKING?

Visit **www.stoplosingcustomersbook.com/resources** for follow-up steps to success.

ACTION STEPS TO BUILDING A WINNING COMMUNICATION STRATEGY:

_____

_____

_____

_____

_____

_____

_____

_____

_____

CHAPTER 9:
HOW TO BUILD A RELATIONSHIP MARKETING CAMPAIGN FOR LEADS AND PROSPECTS

—

I was looking at acquiring a company recently that I'd categorize as a quasi-competitor. I was pretty far into the process: I'd gone through all the financials, and I had taken a look at the products and how they operate. I'd even seen the marketing used to drive the business, and frankly, I was shocked. I couldn't believe that they were doing as well as they were with such bad marketing. The lead generation was crap, and the follow-up was worse. The nurture and prospect education? Nonexistent.

I've bought and sold a handful of companies over the years, and as bad as the marketing was there, it's not the worst I've seen. I also happen to know that how they operate their company is much more common than you'd think.

That may seem like bad news but in reality, it is great news for you and me for a variety of reasons.

The primary reason it is good news for you and me is that with simple relationship marketing campaigns, we can easily outshine even larger competitors.

In the next few chapters, I want to look at how we use relationship marketing to nurture leads and prospects and convert them into paying, loyal customers. If you're up for that, buckle up, as you're in for a wild ride.

Warning!

You may be tempted to skip everything in the previous chapters and just read this one, but if you do that, your relationship marketing campaign won't work.

If you put extra time and resources into getting more customers but haven't fixed the relationship and churn issues from the last few chapters, you can actually end up losing ground faster.

Think about it like this: If you had a machine you used every day to serve your customers and, currently, that machine was being held together by duct tape, some string, and a few used pieces of chewing gum, would it be wise to push that machine even harder? Of course not; the whole thing would simply break. Adding to that, most people go negative on the first few transactions with any new customer, so putting more new customers into a system that is losing them as fast as you can get them will simply decrease profits, increase frustration, and, in extreme cases, even cause the business to go under.

The smartest and safest route is to put these systems and processes in place as prescribed in the book. This will ultimately lead to a more stable and profitable outcome.

Buying From a Relationship Marketer

My first experience with relationship marketing for prospects came in late 2001. Back then, I owned a pair of hot dog stands that were located out in front of two Lowe's Home Improvement stores. I was living in the Bay Area at the time, and as the winter of 2001 was setting in, I realized that it sucked standing outside in the freezing winter weather slinging hot dogs. So, I set out to find another business. Back in 2001, I was only 22 years old, and outside of the hot dog stands and my small high school pager business, I didn't have a ton of real-world business experience. I had always been fascinated by franchises; to me, they appeared to be surefire wins. Not wanting to fail, I went looking for a franchise. My fascination with franchises lead me to actually enjoy reading those franchise disclosure documents (FDD) and other marketing material that any franchiser sends off to prospective franchisees.

As I started my research, I literally inquired on buying over 50 different franchises. All of them sent me their FDD and marketing material. At the time, I was just in the research phase of looking for a new business. As you can imagine, at 22, I wasn't free-flowing with tons of cash and needed to sell both hot dog stands to have any real money to invest in a new business. During the first month after any of my inquiries, I'd get a good amount of follow-up from their salespeople. When I spoke with them, I was 100% upfront with them and said I needed to sell this other business before I could move forward. Within two weeks, most of the salespeople had stopped calling, writing, or emailing. In four weeks, nearly all of them had, and by eight weeks, only one of the over 50 franchises I had inquired about was still attempting to educate me and sell me a franchise.

This one franchiser was named Margo, and she was the CEO of the now-defunct Dry Cleaning To-Your-Door franchise, a pickup-and-delivery dry-cleaning business.

What was Margo's follow-up process? She simply called a few times per month, sent me a monthly eight-page newsletter mainly filled with success stories about existing franchises, and now and again would send me additional articles or informational pieces on why the dry-cleaning business was booming or how pickup-and-delivery was the next big thing.

During many of the phone calls and in some of the newsletters, she'd let me look behind the curtain into her life, and she made a point to ask about my life and girlfriend (now wife). She'd ask how the business was going and if we had any bits on selling. When we sold the first hot dog stand, we even got a congratulations card from her.

About six months after I first inquired, I got a small incentive to buy early from Margo. She asked me if I'd noticed the upcoming franchise convention in Boulder, Colorado. Of course I had, and she told me she thought it would be amazing for me to attend training in June and then the convention before opening my location in July or August. She talked about how successful she thought I'd be and how my market of the Bay Area was ripe for this type of service. She then made me an offer and said, "If you join by the end of the month, you can come to the convention for free."

I did buy, and her offer got me to do it before the end of April. The fact that I didn't keep looking, and at the time wasn't even considering buying from anyone else, is a testament to having good relationship marketing skills and follow-up, but it does beg one question: Where were the other 49-plus franchisers? Isn't a $20,000–$50,000 sale plus 10 years of royalties a good enough reason to follow up with me for six or 12 months? Why did all those franchisers disappear?

The fact of the matter is most people suck at follow-up. Most salespeople and CEOs focus solely on the deals they can close today. That is just plain dumb.

Last year, our follow-up system with leads that are 12 months old or older made over $1.2 million in new annual revenue for The Newsletter Pro. That isn't chump change if you ask me. So many people are leaving massive sums of money on the table, and the fact of the matter is that it isn't too difficult to put a system in place that will get you that money. The best part about this system is that you'll set it up once — which isn't simple but it's not that hard either — and with only minor tweaks implemented now and then, that system will bring you money for many years to come.

"As we've shifted from the old economy to the relationship economy, far too many businesses still don't have effective systems for following up with leads, and frankly, it is costing them dearly."

In the old economy, when a few big players controlled all the information and you had very few choices for suppliers or service providers, the idea of needing a system for good follow-up with leads was crazy. The thought process of the day was if they want to buy, they have to call us. As we've shifted from the old economy to the relationship economy, far too many businesses still don't have effective systems for following up with leads, and frankly, it is costing them dearly.

The funny thing is that to this day, many businesses still don't capture any lead generation info. I can't even imagine. If either poor follow-up or no lead capture describes your business, I have bad news. You've lit a ton of perfectly good cash on fire. Lead capture and nurture is just like planting an oak tree: The best time to plant it was 20 years ago (or whenever you started your business), and the second-best time is today.

Before we go further, I want to be clear on the definition of some of the terms I'm using.

When I say lead, I mean anyone who inquires about buying from you. I don't care if they call, walk in your store, or meet you at a tradeshow or networking event. A lead is anyone who makes an inquiry about buying from you and at least appears (as best as you can tell) to be qualified to do that.

When I talk about lead capture, I'm talking about getting information that will allow you to follow up with and contact that lead in the future. The minimum amount of info you'll need is an email address, but the more info, the better. I prefer leads with full contact info: full name, address, phone or cellphone number, email, and business name. You can also gather qualifying information. For example, at The Newsletter Pro, we want to know how much revenue a lead's business generates, as it helps us know if you're a qualified lead for us or not. You may gather additional information or ask other questions, and that is okay. The more you ask, the lower your response rate will be, but typically the better qualified lead you'll have. At The Newsletter Pro, we don't count anyone as a lead unless we have full contact info. Your definition will vary some, depending on the business you're in.

Another important term is "customer relationship management software," or CRM. I'll go into detail on this a bit later, but a CRM is simply a database that holds all of the information you capture. Most CRM systems also act as marketing automation systems, which allow you to set up systems, tasks, and other activities that the software automatically performs for you. For example, once someone is added as a prospect in your database, the system sends a welcome email on the first day, then, five days later, it sends a follow-up email to the same person without you having to do anything other than set up the system correctly in the first place. They're very powerful tools when used correctly. I'll mention why in a bit, but our preferred vendor for CRM software is at Keap.com.

Now that we are speaking the same language, let's get to work.

DO YOU UNDERSTAND THIS THING CALLED RELATIONSHIP MARKETING YET?

Visit **www.stoplosingcustomersbook.com/resources** for follow-up steps to success.

ACTION STEPS TO TURN YOURSELF INTO A RELATIONSHIP MARKETER:

_____

_____

_____

_____

_____

_____

_____

_____

_____

CHAPTER 10:
THE IMPORTANCE OF NURTURING LEADS

—

Have you ever worked as a server in a restaurant? Odds are you have, whether it was an entry-level job as a teen or a way to put yourself through college. Do you remember how hard the work was and what your strategies were to make great tips? Now, I want you to think of your relationship with a prospect as if it was the relationship between a server and a table of guests.

Imagine you're working in a restaurant when you get the signal from the hostess that a new table is ready for you. You walk over, introduce yourself to the guests, and take their drink orders. So far, things are going great. The diners get a big rush of excitement from meeting you and are happy they'll soon be digging into great food. You've set yourself up for an awesome relationship, but you can't just stop your work there. If you never come back with their drinks or to take their entree orders, you can bet they'll either storm out of the restaurant or you'll lose your table — and your tip — to another waiter.

Taking a drink order and then wandering off is a lot like how most companies sell. They get a lead handed to them, and they respond to that lead but don't follow through. At that point, the prospect is sitting there thinking about the information you gave them, but without more guidance and help, they'll stop participating in your process and most likely find another company to work with.

Now, back to the analogy. Like I said before, if you leave your guests hanging, one of two things will happen. The first option is that you'll lose your table to another waiter. Maybe, when you abandoned the table after taking that first order, those diners flagged down another server and asked about their drinks. If that server promptly returns with their glasses and takes their entree orders, then your table is lost. Why would those diners tip you if you weren't the one taking care of them? All they want is some time and attention. If the diners go with the second option and storm out, the result is the same: They end up at another restaurant where a different server will be nicer to them than you were, and that server gets your tip.

These scenarios are no different than a competitor working on a lead better than you do (or, in the case of the opportunistic waiter, working on stealing one of your customers). Both options ultimately cost you a new sale or an existing customer. Once most businesses get a new customer, they all but forget about that customer. I see it all too often. There isn't any more courting, and things like specials for existing customers go out the window. In fact, there's no more communication at all until it comes time to convince them to buy something or pay the bill. In short, you're not showing them any love. That's like abandoning your table after taking their drink order, then showing up again at the end of the meal to demand your tip.

Now, imagine how differently this scenario could have gone if you employed some relationship marketing and follow-up. In this daydream, not only do you take your table's drink order but you come back with the drinks and do the same with the appetizers, entrees, and desserts.

You even anticipate their needs, keeping an eye on the table from afar so that you can appear at just the right time to refill a drink or take away a dirty plate. At the end of the night, everyone at the table is smiling and they leave you a big, fat tip. Why? Because you gave them your undivided attention. You showed them the love, and it paid off.

If the above info seems simplistic and kind of silly, you're right, it is. Hopefully that means you're ahead of the game, but the reality is that so few are executing properly that most need to go back and up their game because pieces of the puzzle are missing.

The rest of this section will give you the tools to do just that.

Setting Up a Winning Relationship Marketing Campaign for Prospects

As you may have already gathered, I have a different take on running marketing campaigns. Most people want to get the sales part of the process completed as fast as possible. I'm all for closing deals, but I've found that many times, there are massive benefits to slowing the sales process down to give me the opportunity to educate and build a relationship.

Before I build a single campaign, write a single piece of copy, record a video, or even take any action that requires real work, I first ask myself this question: What is my goal?

For example, if you went to my website right now, you'd notice that there is no place to make a purchase on the site. This is intentional. The goal of my site is not to make a sale. The goal is to get people to opt in for a free book, also known as a lead magnet. This is the start of the prospect getting into my funnel and the start of my relationship marketing campaign.

Could I sell directly from my website? Of course, but I'd sell a lot less than if I assume they need information first and aren't ready to buy yet, which is the vast majority of people. The ones who are ready to buy will take additional actions and call/email us, but those who aren't ready to buy right now may be willing to trade their information for something of value. In my case, the item of value is a book on newsletter marketing. It is estimated that only 2%–5% of leads are in the market right now for your product or service. With such a low number of total buyers, it makes sense to play the long game.

Generating Leads vs. Going for the Sale

It is amazing how many parallels dating and generating leads/sales have. Since we're all familiar with dating and dating etiquette, they make good analogies for explaining the proper way to lead generate and close sales. Here is my favorite one for lead generation.

You're out with some friends for a night on the town, and halfway through the night, one of your friends sees the girl of his dreams. He stops nearly dead in his tracks when he first catches a glimpse of her. Your friend grabs your arm and points to a very beautiful woman standing near the bar. He then tells you, "I'm going to marry this girl." You laugh, and next thing you know, your friend is walking over to the bar where this woman is standing. You catch up to him just as he walks up, interrupts the woman, and introduces himself, and right after she introduces herself back, your buddy drops to one knee and asks her to marry him. He explains that she is the most beautiful woman he has ever seen and that he knows they're soulmates. Stunned at first, the woman looks at her friends, laughs at your buddy, and walks away. You spend the evening consoling your buddy.

Fortunately, or maybe unfortunately (after all, it could be funny to watch in person), I've never had the privilege of witnessing this in a dating situation, but I do watch businesses do this all the time.

They put an ad up and show it to a cold group of prospects and ask those prospects to buy. When no one buys, they blame the media, the copy, or anyone but themselves. It's crazy town.

Now, if we look at the same situation where your buddy sees the girl of his dreams and lead generates instead of going straight for the sale, the outcome is different.

You're out with some friends for a night on the town, and halfway through the night, one of your friends sees "the girl of his dreams." He stops nearly dead in his tracks when he first catches a glimpse of her. Your friend grabs your arm and points to a very beautiful woman standing near the bar. He then tells you, "I'm going to marry this girl." You laugh, and next thing you know, your friend is walking over to the bar where the girl of his dreams is standing. You catch up and get to him just as he walks up and interrupts the woman. He introduces himself and simply asks to buy her a drink. She laughs and says, "Okay." You play a good wingman and buy her friend a drink, and at the end of the evening, your buddy exchanges numbers with the girl of his dreams.

A few weeks pass, and your buddy and the girl of his dreams start dating. Within six months, they're married and live happily ever after.

The second scenario isn't that far off from actual stories I've heard happy couples tell.

The first story, though, is how most businesses operate with their leads.

Lead Magnets for the Win!

It is very common for people to get stuck trying to figure out what lead magnet to create and how to best use it. This book isn't designed to be all-inclusive training on lead magnets, but I'd be doing you a disservice if I didn't have some solid info for you to use to create or improve on an existing lead magnet.

I have three very important rules for you to remember when creating lead magnets.

1. **It may not work, and that's okay.** You may not knock it out of the park the first time at-bat. Don't worry about it. If you've ever played sports, you know no one is amazing the first time they try anything. LeBron James likely missed many shots in pee-wee basketball. You, too, are likely to miss many shots. Don't sweat it; just pick the ball up and try again.
2. **Make sure you add value.** I've seen some garbage lead magnets that barely, if at all, live up to the hype of the copy convincing you to opt in for them. Don't be that guy. It will start the relationship off on the wrong foot.
3. **Your lead magnet shouldn't take days or weeks to consume.** Don't try to give them a hangover on the first date. One or two drinks will do.

What Should You Use as a Lead Magnet?

Books are awesome and work well, but if you want to get something up and working a lot faster than you could write and publish a book, you have a few options.

Let's start with cold prospecting. Cold prospecting would be a situation where you create an ad and place it in a media. For example, Facebook and magazine ads are examples of cold prospecting. The prospect who is consuming the content on Facebook or in a magazine didn't go there or buy that magazine to find your ad. Instead, they went there to get an update on what's going on with their friends or the latest celebrity gossip. When you're targeting prospects, you need to create a lead magnet that helps them solve a problem that your customers face 30, 60, or 90 days out from when they plan on doing business with you.

If we continue to use The Newsletter Pro as our example company here, a book on newsletter marketing isn't going to work well with cold prospecting. It is unlikely people logged onto Facebook hoping they'd see an ad to find out about newsletters.

But my prospects 90 days out may be concerned with churn in their business. They are not likely to click on an ad that is all about newsletters because they don't yet know that newsletters can help reduce churn via relationship marketing. But what if I showed them a free report on the top seven reasons why a patient switches dentists and what to do to stop the bleeding (no pun intended)? If my targeting was right and I was showing that to a dentist and the dentist was aware they have a churn issue, they would be much more likely to click and opt in to get the information.

Inside my report, I include the information I promised along with the next steps and a call to action.

Some of the best lead magnets are the ones that give results in advance. I love using this strategy. When people take your advice and have a successful outcome, it builds your relationship with them fast. Once you've proven you're the real deal and done it for free, it isn't a huge leap for prospects to consider buying your products or services.

Of course, it is possible that someone gets your lead magnet, reads your info, sees your call to action, and decides they are now ready to buy. The problem is it is not probable. It is much more probable that you will have to do more education, nurturing, and relationship-building to get your lead to convert, but the good news is we got a lead.

Remember that getting more information from a prospect is better as long as it doesn't destroy conversions. If you run into a situation where you need five pieces of data and that destroys the conversions, you have to either fix the copy, fix the lead magnet, or start over. You typically don't want to take less information than you need, but you also don't want to ask for the world and not get a single opt-in. I hate to say it, but the truth is that you'll have to test it.

Once you have the lead and they have their info, a bonus option for you is to either sell something on the thank-you page where they download their lead magnet or offer additional training, which is what we do. I prefer that the training be on the same subject or very similar to the report they just downloaded, but that is not a hard-and-fast rule. It will typically amount to more people consuming the training, though. I know some people add in a webinar offer where the person has to register for another event. Personally, I don't think this works as well as a video-on-demand training. The lead is hot and interested right there, right now. Let's help them scratch that itch and, in the process, educate them about our products and services.

If you're in a service-based business or retail, you may think this doesn't apply to you. Think again. You have customers who come and go all the time, so wouldn't it be valuable to have a means to communicate with them and a list of who they are?

If you're a restaurant and are having a slow week, wouldn't it be nice if, because you gave your customers and prospective customers a lead magnet, you were able to get their contact info and simply email or text them a promotion?

If you're a dentist, couldn't you use a lead magnet to attract larger cases? For example, the lead magnet is the seven dangers of implants that no dentist will tell you about. Of course, spin some of those negatives into positives for doing business with your practice, so that if the prospect compares you to any other dentist, the other dentist simply won't be able to measure up.

One option some people use is to have prospects pay a small fee for the lead magnet. I've seen this done, and some folks swear by it, but many entrepreneurs do it wrong.

What I've seen business owners do is try to offer a $7–$10 product, but instead of making a great product with massive value, they simply start charging for their existing lead magnet. When you charge, you will see far fewer leads, but in theory, the leads you get will be more qualified. I'm not opposed to charging for a lead magnet, but in my experience, you have to amp up the value. If I'm going to charge you $7, I want the value of the information you're buying to be worth at least $70. That doesn't mean you simply say it is worth $70 dollars; you have to actually justify the price tag and reasonably believe someone would give you $70 for that info.

A perfect example of this is the old Columbia House Records promotion of "get 10 CDs for a penny with a commitment to buy seven more in the next 12 months at full price." This is a crazy irresistible offer. I know I participated more than once in that deal. The value is far greater than the penny I'm paying; people happily paid the penny and the shipping charges and bought seven more CDs at full price. It was a no-brainer. Any lead magnet you charge for should be a no-brainer once the prospect realizes the value you're providing them.

Nurture Campaigns

A nurture campaign is a campaign that is designed to provide information and add value to the prospects' lives while moving them toward a purchase and, when appropriate, asking the prospect to make a purchase.

I approach creating a nurture campaign with three things in mind.

1. **How can I deepen my relationship with this prospect?**
2. **What is the next action I need the prospect to take?**
3. **What type of education does the prospect need before they will buy from me?**

If I focus on deepening the relationship with both personal and professional information and my calls to action are ones that move the prospect to the next step, I have a winning campaign.

It isn't an accident that relationship is No. 1 on the above list. Don't misunderstand me; I want to make the sale as much as the next guy, but if I get you on my list and then spam you to buy, it won't take long before any trust I've built up is gone and I forever live in your spam folder.

You have to make sure you are adding value in between the times you're asking for money.

Looking at how we do things at The Newsletter Pro again, we run our first nurture campaign for 90 days, and it includes phone calls, emails, text messaging, and direct mail.

Don't make the common mistake of thinking you need 90 days worth of emails, direct mail, and phone scripts to start. You only need *three* emails to start. You can add a new one each week and a direct mail campaign in two weeks. You'll have your weekend reading set, which will give you another email where you can add value once per week. You also want to put your prospects on your newsletter list. This is often overlooked, and it is costing businesses massive amounts of money in lost sales.

After the 90 days, if they haven't taken the action we desire, my goal switches to re-engagement.
The goal of re-engagement is to get you top of mind with the prospect again and to try to help them with a different problem because the first issue didn't get them moving.

At The Newsletter Pro, if you got the lead magnet on churn, we'd then offer you a new lead magnet on referrals, with the goal being to get you to opt in for that and start down that campaign for the next 90-plus days.

If you still don't respond, we may offer you a third lead magnet or offer you something of value for a very low price, as we described above.

We continue to cycle you through lead magnets, offers, and other nurture emails until you buy, die, or unsubscribe.

Now that you have all the necessary knowledge to develop a lead nurturing campaign, you need to incorporate the most important part of this process: the CRM. I've said this before in this book and I'll say it again: The only way to win the relationship marketing game is with organization and automation, so you have to have a system in place to properly record your lead generation process. Once you have the know-how to build an effective nurture campaign and a CRM system to execute it, you'll be well on your way to being a true relationship marketer.

HOW ARE YOU NURTURING LEADS AND PROSPECTS?

Visit **www.stoplosingcustomersbook.com/resources**
for follow-up steps to success.

ACTION STEPS TO CONVERT THEM INTO PAYING, LOYAL CUSTOMERS:

_____

_____

_____

_____

_____

_____

_____

_____

_____

CHAPTER 11:
THE ONLY THING YOUR COMPETITORS CAN'T COPY IS YOU

—

There are few things all entrepreneurs can agree on, but one is this universal fact: Owning a business is extremely difficult. No matter what you've read in this book or any other, there is no easy solution to your struggle, regardless of your industry. All the strategies, tools, and tactics you've read about in this book take work to implement and even more effort after that to produce results.

Of course, you'd never have started your business if you had a subpar work ethic. You got to where you are today because you worked hard for it. The problem is that so many people get to your level then fail because of outdated marketing. Folks, it's almost 2020, and we are in the relationship economy. That means you have to show your customers *why* you've worked so hard to get where you are. You have to pull back the curtain to reveal yourself, your aspirations, and your devotion to your customers and your company. This isn't easy, but I can't emphasize it enough. Today's customers buy from people and companies they know. If you don't take advantage of the opportunity to show your customers who you are, you'll be shooting your own company in the foot and opening your doors to the competition.

No matter how much you grow, competitors will always try to elbow their way into your share of the market. At this stage, nearly 100% of businesses are new commodities. All of your competitors basically do the same thing you do, and even if they don't, they can cheerfully spin it so the market thinks they do. It's unfortunate, but it's the truth. Still, no one knows better than you what sets your services apart. If you're anything like me, then you became an entrepreneur because you wanted to do things a different way: your way. And there's no doubt in your mind that your way is the best way.

When it comes to proving that to your customers, nothing is more effective than sharing who you are. In order to do that well, you have to believe in relationship marketing and the relationship economy. I've given you plenty of reasons why you should in this book, but you're the one who has to take the concept and use it to increase sales, keep customers, and grow the success of your business. Once you build that confidence in your new marketing campaigns, then you can create a comprehensive relationship marketing system to propel your business forward.

Here's the simple truth: No matter who or how big your competition is, the only thing they can't copy is *you* — your brand stories and the relationships you have with your customers, vendors, and partners. They can try, and they may even swipe an idea or two, but a true customer relationship and experience system is nearly impossible to duplicate. In the business world today, uniqueness is your most important advantage. When you showcase your uniqueness, something amazing happens: You form a relationship, which the most valuable asset an entrepreneur can hope to acquire.

In my own relationship marketing, I include important parts of who I am to paint a picture of myself for my clients. In our newsletter at The

Newsletter Pro, for example, I always include excerpts from Scripture that were powerful and motivating for me that month. I know not everyone in my target demographic believes in the Christian faith, but my spirituality is central to my identity, so I'm not being my authentic self in my copy if I omit my connection to God. That said, spirituality isn't all of who I am. If I think they fit well in an article, I might drop Cardi B lyrics into the same newsletter where I've included an excerpt from Corinthians, just because I like her music. After I send out those newsletters, I don't get responses from every one of my readers, but those who do reach out always sing the praises of such personal details.

As I've shown over and over in this book, to be a great company, you have to focus on the customer relationship as well as the customer experience. The market is shifting, and over the next few years, I predict we'll see more and more sad stories about companies going out of business after decades of success because they didn't make the transition. Of course, even more businesses will close that never make the news. People will blame those closures on all the typical things — they ran out of money, management was poor, etc. — but in many cases, the real reason for their failure will be a lack of focus on the customer experience and relationship.

As I said before, relationship marketing isn't easy, but nothing worth doing ever is. Will you refuse to dig in, choosing the path of so many long-lost businesses and retailers, only to find yourself out of business or struggling to make ends meet? Or will you choose to invest in relationship marketing and create the experiences and relationships that will put your business on track for success?

The choice, ultimately, is yours. Choose wisely.

HAVE YOU LOST YOUR "WHY"?

Visit **www.stoplosingcustomersbook.com/resources** for follow-up steps to success.

ACTION STEPS TO RECONNECT WITH YOUR BUSINESS'S PURPOSE:

_____

_____

_____

_____

_____

_____

_____

_____

Printed in Great Britain
by Amazon

11011393R00078